Illuminations of Love

Romantic Musings, Volume III

Matthew A Cone

FORESMAN
PUBLICATIONS

An imprint of Foresman Publications
ForesmanPublications.com

Printed in the United States of America

ISBN: 979-8-9906678-7-7

To My Muse

You became my Muse

Beautiful, my life changed so much after I met you that day

I had never met someone like you before

Now I have been changed in so many way, I am no longer the same

Opening my heart to you took so much effort to allow you in

After many years of struggling to find someone who would love me for me

All those years turned me into someone I didn't want to be, but then I met you

You became the inspiration of my life, the purpose for my words

I have never been open with my thoughts and my emotions, until you

You gave me courage to open up about my feelings of love and pain

I will never be the same since I met you, I feel again, after years of silence

You allowed me to find my voice within the written word, sharing with others

You gave me courage to be open about my feelings of love and pain

You became my strength in that moment you opened my heart again

You became an inspiration within your eyes as you led me towards opening my heart

You became my Muse, the one person that fully believed in me, healing my self-doubt

I had hidden from the world, I have been filled with fear, to share my heart with others

I have kept my words locked away, until you opened my heart to share

I never knew strength until I found you in my arms, loving you as you believe in me

Musings by M

Contents

Chapters 1 & 2

Illuminations of Love

Romantic Musings

Matthew A Cone

can be found in Volume One
of Illuminations of Love

Chapters 3-6

can be found in Volume Two
of Illuminations of Love

Chapter Seven

When You Entered My Life

W hen you tell me you love me I still pause on the words

They touch me deep within even to this day just three words

I love you, said by the right person can change my day completely

When you show me you love me I am still in shock of what you do

Taking burdens from me and making my life a bit lighter and freeing me

From the stress of always having to be the person others rely on

When you touch me I pause in the moment we have just shared together

Still to this day, your touch sends a wave of joy and peace through all of me

Your soft skin against my arm or hand can melt my stress quickly away

When you kiss me I relish the touch and taste of your lips on mine

A kiss from you offered freely takes my breath away I crave it always

Your lips on mine, quickly touching mine or lingeringly elevates my heart and day

When you speak to me a voice of an angel is what I hear every time I hear it

From the day we met to this day it will never change it is music to my ears

The laughter in your voice always lifts my heart and soul skyward

When you came into my life, my life changed, and it continues to get better each day

Each day with you is a miracle of love and life shared with one so amazing and strong

Life has been a struggle, yet the purity of your heart has always found its way outward

Musings by M

Occasionally, I hesitate to add anything to one of the musings because it feels like it could detract from the reader's perception. I waited to place this note here so that you, as the reader, could experience this musing without any influence from me. M

The Rose

Every petal of a rose represents the feelings of love

As you present your love a rose, it shows your love for them

It brings a smile to both of you as you express your love

Flowers are always nice, but a rose can mean much more

A red rose is a rose given to show the love for another

A white rose is a rose of everlasting love for another

A yellow rose is a rose that means there is friendship

A black rose is a rose that has multiple meanings

Then there is your rose, Lavender or purple for some

A beautiful rose of enchantment or the mystery of love

You love them and I love to give them to you, a special rose

The smile on your lips as you take one from me is amazing

A red rose like your lips as you speak and smile at me

Glorious and bright, beautiful, and sweet to the touch

A white rose like the purity of the love we feel for each other

As we grow each day together, our love grows as well

A yellow rose is the sunlight you brought into my life

From so much darkness into the light of the love you give

A black rose is the color of your hair, as it hangs over your shoulders

Up or down your hair frames your beautiful face

A lavender rose, mystical and enchanting it is who you are to me

When I met you my life changed and became so much more than before

A love that will never end between us lasting far beyond what I have known

Once so rare for me I found the one precious love I searched for so long

Musings by M

Flowers for most people hold a special place in each heart and when it comes to a rose, most agree they are special. Each color expresses different feelings and emotions from the giver to the one receiving the rose. Receiving flowers, not just from the grocery store, can mean the giver took extra time and effort to make the receiver's day happier. Ladies, would you agree? M

We Collided

We collided one day between the stars and remain connected even now

Through all the tumbling and the twists and turns we have experienced

We are here today joined with love, joined in purpose, joined forever

When we collided, I was on a path of self-destruction not caring for anything

When you entered my life I finally saw hope of a life in love again with you

You changed my direction in my life with the love you gave to me I have changed

We have not had an easy story, but it has been a story of survival and of strength

Of two people coming together in a world where everyone and everything is against them

Yet here we stand hand in hand side by side, bruised, battered but not beaten

We are together against the odds that said we would never last yet here we are

You have given strength I never knew I possessed, pulling from deep within my soul

I have walked, held you, comforted you and you have done the same for me

We are bound together by a force greater than ourselves our love will never die

Life for us has never been an easy path to take, without our love we would have failed

Musings by M

When you least expect it, someone will enter your life and completely change it. This can be a mentor, a friend or a lover. They reveal something you may have missed in your life. We change because we recognize the need for change, and this connection leads us to new insights, experiences, and understanding of the life we are meant to live.

Damaged Goods (Lyrics)

Mornings, you look in the mirror and think about you

You see only brokenness, someone who isn't worthy

Worthless, alone, not lovable enough

You don't see the truth of who you are to so many

The one who gives so much to make others better

When you see yourself as only damaged goods

For so long, no one showed you the reality of you

They have judged you, abused you, tried to destroy you

You can't see who you are to those who really know

What you have had to endure for so long, it's your past

It's the way you were taken advantage of, not loved

You passed through life thinking you were nothing

Mornings, you look in the mirror and think about you

You see only brokenness, someone who isn't worthy

Worthless, alone, not loveable enough

You don't see the truth of who you are to so many

The one who gives so much to make others better

When you see yourself as only damaged goods

So many nights suffering from doubts and fears

Your dreams only bringing you more of the same

The nightmares, the terror of your thoughts, waking you

Your heart pounding, you are covered in sweat from
what you see

You try to stay awake, hoping you don't have to relive it

But as your eyes close again, it's all back and it begins again

Mornings, you look in the mirror and think about you

You see only brokenness, someone who isn't worthy

Worthless, alone, not loveable enough

You don't see the truth of who are to so many

The one who gives so much to make others better

When you see yourself as only damaged goods

You try to scream, but there's only silence, nothing heard

Your mind tries to protect you from the torture of your past

But it just keeps coming back night after night, nothing helps

The doctors give you one pill after another to fight the terror

Knowing this only numbs the torture, the terror in your mind

You close your eyes, praying it works this time, but it starts again

Mornings, you look in the mirror and think about you

You see only brokenness, someone who isn't worthy

Worthless, alone, not loveable enough

You don't see the truth of who are to so many

The one who gives so much to make others better

When you see yourself as only damaged goods

Musings by M

I wrote this with someone in mind. Someone who is so amazing but doesn't see themselves as amazing. Someone who has been mistreated for so long that they don't see themselves as anything but damaged goods. They are special yet think they have no value. Many go through life, not realizing how truly amazing they are because they have only been told they are worthless or must do something to earn another's love. Damaged by life and others, they think they are just damaged goods. M

From the Beginning

Thinking of who would be perfect for me, to have in my life

The one who will know me the best, understand my moods

I was wondering if there was really someone who was like that

Then I met you, such an amazing person, someone who loves

As I have thought of who you might be, I heard your voice and knew

I knew from the sound of your intelligence, your personality came through

I knew I had to get to know the person whose voice I was hearing

Then I saw you for the first time and it was even a stronger pull to you

I needed to get to know you better, you needed to get to know me too

We spent time together and this desire I had grew and it grew for you

Our first kiss lingers in my mind, the feel of our lips touching, electrifying

I knew again that you were the one who would love me, because I love you

Love can be fickle at times, it can go low and it can go high again, ours was high

It was like I had been drugged with love for you; it continues to this day, intoxicating

You have shown me that love can be strong, it can last through issues as they arrive for us

Your love for me has cured the brokenness I had always known, trying to love someone

Now, even when we are apart, you are the one I long to have near me, to hold you

To feel your arms around me, to give me the strength to face all of life's trials together

Knowing you are near me, it gives me the courage to face my own demons from the past

Allowing me to look to a future with hope, with love, with knowing you are there

Musings by M

After love has failed to protect us because it has broken us, when we face each day with our guard up to love, we stop looking for love. Someone enters our lives and shows us love, a type of love that helps us heal. Giving us unconditional love, something we have never known. It takes time for the brokenness to heal, but with care and consistent love we have never known, healing will begin. M

When You Came Into My Life

W hen you came into my life, I had no idea how much you would change me

I saw a beautiful woman before me the day we met, a lady I wanted to know

As we got to know each other, I knew you were the woman, the only one for me

When you came into my life, I wondered if you would even want to get to know me

We became inseparable, we laughed and enjoyed so many amazing days and nights

We worked side by side, we became a couple, and our love grew from a crush to love

When you came into my life, you slowly took the hurt and anger away from my heart and mind

You began to fill the spaces with a love I had never known, one that was strong and lasting

I remember the first kiss we shared. I was so amazed at the passion I could feel for another

When you came into my life, I wanted to share time with you, and we did from that day forth

We were never too far away from each other on the phone, in our thoughts, and in our hearts

I fell in love with you from the moment we met, you took my breath away, replacing it with love

When you came into my life, I became someone else, not by force, because of the love you gave me

I felt the change you brought into my life, and I learned to love unconditionally in my love for you

Our love is perfect for us and will always be our love, not shared with anyone else

Musings by M

She came into my life, and I am grateful for her love, changing me. Because of her, I started writing again. Because of her, I now know what unconditional love really means. Thank you, lady, for loving me and helping me to change with your love.

Broken Hearts

B roken hearts can always heal from the pain that's left

The pain of loss can be taken away if there is love

When we lose a friend, a family member, or a love

It takes time, it takes love, it takes courage to stand firm

It can be hard as hell to take that step forward to move

A love that changes your life can bring healing back to us

If they stepped away from us, they could come back

To rekindle the healing love for us, for a future together again

Open and honest love is always open to those who matter most

Family and celebrate the union of this love, they support it

It can take time, it takes forgiving each other for what might have happened

Love, real love, can change the past and balance the future of love

The passion can return for each, the love lights the path to love again

But how this will happen is up to each to decide the path they will walk

Will we each give love another chance to blossom and grow?

How will we write the rest of our story now?

Musings by M

In love, trust is precious and necessary to the love that is shared. Love will be lost when trust is lost, but healing can occur. Healing of broken hearts takes time, patience, and a willingness to forgive. Not always easy. Not always possible, but it can happen. M

My Daughter

I may not have carried you before

But I'm holding you close now

Never facing the world alone again

You, my daughter, have a home in my heart

I will never leave you; you are mine

I loved you from the first day we met

You walked into my life, Daughter

I knew you will not face life alone again

Never alone again, we are family now

You are not my blood, you are my heart

I am your mom and will always be

You are not alone in this world, my daughter

I believe in you; I am your biggest fan, amazing child

You captured this momma's heart, so much love

For a daughter who is so amazing, so beautiful

You are never alone again, it's my promise to you

Side by side, we will fight the pains of life together

We will stand and face the world as one, you and I

No more broken hearts, love will prevail through it all

You will never face another day of life alone, my daughter

Musings by M

When a mom takes in a child who has been abandoned by everyone else, the love bond grows quickly between them. That child is seeking acceptance from a parent who has never received it. The bond of life and love lingers throughout the lives of both, never to fade. I never knew this myself, but I have seen it in the lives of women I know. This is entitled as it is for a special Mother and daughter I know who share a special bond. M

A Million Reasons Why

People have asked me why I love you, as if I need to justify why

But I never hesitate to tell them the reason why I do love you

Never has there been a woman like you who has entered my life before

You have brought me back to life and shown me what real love is again

I have felt the deep emotional feelings we share with one another from the start

It has been a challenge for me to understand why you love me, but then I smile

When I am near you, I can still feel the sparks between us; you and I are electric

We have faced many challenges, yet here we stand as one, facing them head-on

When I am away from you, the love I have for you simmers until we are joined again

When I think of you, a smile comes to my eyes, and the butterflies begin anew

Never have I felt the power of love, a love that has carried me for all these years

That supports and nourishes my soul's desires and the cravings for your touch

I have been asked why I love you the way I do, and it is easy to explain the million reasons why

But then I stop and ask the person why they need to know the reasons why I love you so

Our love has been a rollercoaster of emotions, feelings of joy, and some sorrow

But through it all, I have never doubted that our love will last a lifetime, strong and unbreakable

Musings by M

There is no need to justify why we love someone to others as long as it makes sense to both of you. But we can always find the words to express why we love them. M

Your Eyes

So many thoughts as I sit here right now, I am trying to sort them all out
I want to hold you in my arms and look into your eyes, Spellbound lovers
I want to gaze into your eyes to see the love you share with me, my love
Many times, words can mask feelings one has for another, yet eyes speak the truth

Eyes never lie, they cannot lie, even when words can sound hollow or too profound
You have been the one who tried to convince others that you are so in control of life
I look into your eyes and can see the fear you hold deep within your heart and mind
I know you well, I can hear your words, my love, but your eyes cannot lie to me

I see you looking around, watching everyone and everything around you, constantly scanning
But when you look into my eyes, I see the one I fell in love with, all the strength and fear
All the love you have to share with others, and thankfully, I am the one you share it with
Even though things are not always the way we had envisioned our love, we make it work

Your eyes, so deep and inviting, when you feel at peace away from the torment of life
Eyes so full of a passion that it can take my breath away, as if you are drinking me in
Fixated on your eyes, I am drawn into your world, the chaos, the peace of your life
Like I am in a trance, I move towards you, caught in your web of love, ready to devour me

I have never known anyone like you before, a woman who loves without holding back
Life was never easy for either one of us; you have a fierceness and a softness within you
The passion in your eyes is unlike a look I have seen before in the eyes of such an amazing woman
I am amazed every day that I am the lucky one to feel your love, the one you choose to love

Musings by M

The eyes, windows to the soul, they say. Eyes don't lie, even when people try to convince themselves that everything is okay. Eyes always tell the truth about what we try to hide from ourselves and others. Look into your lover's eyes and ask them deep and, at times, difficult questions. Their eyes will speak the truth before their words are even spoken. M

Show Your Love Daily

How can we show someone we genuinely love them in just one day

If we really love someone, it will take more than one year to show our love

Too many people think one day a year is enough to show our love for someone

I have heard Valentine's Day referred to as forced affection day or singles day

Why would we stop on just one day a year to show them we love them

Why not every day of each month, for years to come, to show how much we love them

One day will never tell the story of the love we have for someone or they have for us

One day cannot even begin to show someone we love them and care about them

One day is just not enough time for love to grow and flourish, growing daily deeper in love

Don't let the love you have for your special person be solely shown in just one day

If we love someone, truly love someone, we will show them every day, not just with words

But with actions, acts of service, little notes spread throughout the day, written or texted

When we get home, we will make sure they are shown our love through talking and sharing our day

We will ask questions, we will laugh, we will help with whatever needs help, maybe a bubble bath

Why would we stop at just one day a year to show our love to someone? Why not every day of the year

If we truly love someone, if they have our heart and soul, we will show them every day

We will never stop showing them that we love them above all others, never wanting them to doubt

Love shown all year means more than just one day; it creates a safe place where love always grows

Musings by M

Valentine's Day is more than a single day; it should be year-round. Some see it as a day of forced affection, when people must show others they care for and love. If there is love for another, why not show it year-round? Every day should be Valentine's Day. M

Your Warmth Shines Through

As we walk along snow-covered lanes, I am aware of the eyes upon you

The wonder they show me as you pass through the winter cold around us

They look upon you with wonder, as your beauty shines through

Even now, as you speak, the cold tries to freeze your words within it

Yet you, of all the ones upon this lane, have a way of bringing hope of tomorrow

A love that reaches even the coldest of hearts, bringing joy with every word

Your eyes sparkle with love for those you meet, warming them within

There are the reflections of stars as you look around and see each one

Never has there been an angel sent from above with so much to give to others

The smile you share with each one leaves a sweetness never known

As you speak, your words reach deep within, your spirit shines through

The cold all around seems to fade away, even if just for a moment

In the depths of this frigid cold, you bring a glimmer of the spring to come

A time of renewal and hope for the return of growth and life once again

Within this heart of mine, I have felt it, with just the touch of your hand

All eyes are upon you as your radiance warms even the coldest of hearts

The winter fears your warm and caring smile, yet you share it with all you encounter

Never shying away from giving hope to others, taking their burdens away for a while

Musings by M

Even within the ravages of a bitter cold winter's day, there are those who, by just existing, can bring a warmth to thaw even the coldest of nights. With eyes that sparkle and a smile that warms. As their words of calming peace are spoken, they are like the warmth of a softly glowing fire, warming all they encounter. M

I'm So Proud of You

I am so proud of you and everything you have done

Not everyone could have overcome the things you fought

It has drained your spirit and caused you such pain and anguish

I am so proud of you and the way you see the world around you

You have a spirit, though weakened, it has never been broken by pain

You have stood up and turned away the abuse, the insults, the hate

I am so proud of you for the way you have raised the children with love

Many would take the pain out on the children, but you have chosen love

Loving them even though you were in so much pain and feeling worthless

I am so proud of you, no one understands the things you have been put through

Yet you face every day with a renewed hope of a better day, one of peace

One day, you will find peace within your life, finally finding true joy

I am so proud of you for your resolve, for your sarcastic mouth, your humor

I am so proud of you, even if no one else will tell you they are proud of your strength

I am so proud of you and all you have overcome, a fighter to the end, yet so loving

Musings by M

I am sure we all know someone to whom this can fit. It could be us as well. Remember that the path they have struggled on was a path they had to walk, mostly alone, but others may have walked it by their side. Let them know we are proud of them for making it to the point of healing; some are still healing. Tell them why we are proud of them. They need to hear it. M

Your Heart is Golden

I have stood by your side all these years, adoring you, my love

As I watch you struggle with the thoughts of everything you have faced

From hate to sadness, you hold deep inside that heart of yours

Through all the struggles to make sense of the pain others have put you through

You have tried, your whole life, to make sense of why they caused you to hurt so badly

Those you thought you could trust, those you thought had loved you so

You have tried to comprehend the sorrow, the feelings of loneliness, and so much loneliness

Never have you given in to the anger that you at times feel within your heart and mind

You give love to those you see every day, to the ones who have suffered the same as you

Your heart is golden, yet it should be stone; your heart is open, though it should be closed

You look to help those who have suffered at the hands of others, the same as you have

And yet no one knows the depth of pain and sorrow you fight against every day

You fight every day to understand why the pain was inflicted upon you so young

There is not a night that goes by when your dreams don't turn to nightmares of the past.

Yet as dawn breaks, you force a smile onto your beautiful face, masking the pain within

As I have stood by you, I am amazed you can love the way you love, after all the pain

Instead of hate, you show love to those around you, compassion pouring from your soul

Even as you struggle to understand your pain, you love the children of this world, shielding them

Musings by M

When we stand by someone healing from past traumas and pain, we should support them through their work. Just being there for them as they need us helps. They will work through their push-pull situations as the healing will bring them more pain, helping them heal and overcome their past. Love them through it, and please understand they are healing; this is the process they must go through. M

Never Knew Love

I never knew love until I found you, the day I did, a breath of fresh air, a newness unknown

I had searched for a love I could hold in my arms; we soon became one, a love and a friend

I cherish every day with you by my side, there is not a moment that goes by that I don't feel your love

You entered my life and changed my heart, you opened it up and filled it with so much joy

You became the center of my life, the hope I had lost long ago, the desire to be better, I forgot

You took my hand and led me to a place of peace, showed me there was more to me

Our days have been spent speaking on the phone, texting, and holding our love together

Our nights are spent with the love we share and showing each other the passion, we feel

Our world has become filled with the warmth of the love we share for each other

We have become so intertwined, so connected, and full of the life we both wanted for so long

We now know there was a love waiting for us that finally became the love we share; so amazing

We looked for so long for a love that would change us and our world, now we know true love

I never knew love until I found you the day I did, there is not a moment that goes by I don't feel your love

You entered my life, took my hand, and led me to the hope I had lost long ago, and led me to a place of peace

We looked so long for a love that would change us and fill us with the warmth of the love we share

Life and the desire to find someone who will love us for who we are, not for what we can do for them. Then, we need to find someone who sees our imperfections yet still loves all of us. When we find the one, life changes for us and them. Then we can work to ensure we never lose each other. Yes, a love like this takes work and acceptance. It is so worth it. M

Our Life and Love

You saved me from the pain I once felt so deeply within my heart

You came into my life and showed me I was more than the pain

You took away the loneliness I have lived with for so long

I finally found someone who loved me despite the pain I have endured

I finally know that I can be better than everyone told me I was in their eyes

I can look at myself in the mirror and realize I am worth more than I thought

With you in my world, I know there is more to me than I heard I was before you

With you in my life, I know there is a life just waiting for me to live at last

With you by my side, I understand there is a love for even me to feel finally

As we face the trials we will face in the future, we will be here for each other

As we face the pain of the struggles we will face, together, the same

As we look for hope, we will find it within the love we share together

Musings by M

There is one person who will see you for who you really are and love you despite your scars and bruises. One person who sees beyond the pain that life has put you through. They will love you for you, not your past. M

We Are Meant to Be

W e are meant to be a part of each other's lives, and fate has seen to it

Never to know another lonely day or night, our lives intertwined

Whether as just friends or staying as lovers, we are here until the end

We are meant to help each other, to be the strength when weakness sets in

Giving hope and joy to each other, the power to stand side by side

At times, holding each other, supporting, and encouraging each other in the face of the pain

We are meant to allow love to shine through, even within the darkest of times

Showing each one the love longed for, the peace so long sought but never found

Time will tell if the strength of the love we share will last until the end

We are meant to light the way, adding the love that we have, giving of ourselves

Never holding back, the passion or the love, once buried so deep within our hearts

Allowing ourselves to love fully the one we stand with now, never walking away

Musings by M

Friends and lovers, some people are meant to be together. They have been brought into each other's lives to stand together. Fighting off the world and standing side by side. They were meant to meet and help one another. Together, they feel each other's strength. If love grows from it, the love is more profound and stronger. The world will know they will bring a truth some might be fearful of but needed. M

Can You Feel My Love?

C an you feel my love for you when I close my eyes and think of you

The depth of the feelings I feel within my heart for you

I have never known anyone like you; the depth of my love for you scares me

Do you feel my heart beating with this love I have for you; every beat is yours

This love I have for you keeps my heart moving, keeping me alive with desire

Knowing you healed my brokenness, the pieces are whole again within my heart

Do you feel the peace I have within this love we share? I now know peace in my life

Even when we are apart, there is a feeling of tranquility within me that I have never felt

Knowing your heart and mine beat as one, beat by beat, they feel the love we share

We were meant to find each other and heal each other through the love we share together

Both of us have faced chaos our entire lives, yet within the chaos, we find our peace as one

Can you feel the calmness of this love as we face the hate of the world around us, within our love

Though we have never known wholeness before as we have faced life, we are finally whole

Within this love we share, the bond we have has never been broken

As we grow within the circle of our love, we can know there is nothing that will break us apart

Musings by M

Even during times apart, we long for the loved one not by our side. The separation can make us long for the other. We close our eyes and see them in our minds. Do they feel our love flowing to them? M

Healng Beat by Beat

R ight you, but it was the wrong time for us to become our forever

You are the world I want to create, the one I want by my side to the end

When they lay me below the surface of this world, by me, for our time

Right me, but my brokenness was too fractured; we both needed to heal

For the love we both deserve and want, it will be ours to hold in the end

When I take my last breath, there within the faces I will see is yours

Right us, two people fighting our past to build our future, our forever

With our broken hearts, the healing our love can bring us

But the healing needs to be our individual healing before we come together

Right love, but the time for us will have to wait until the healing is completed

Healed, we can love each other the way we want and deserve, the past gone, then

Just our future within the love we deserve, whole, healthy, and deeply spiritual

Right you, right me, right us, right love, soon it will be for me and you

Healthy and healed, our love is still strong, even apart, it is within us

Simmering, growing in the recesses of our broken hearts, healing beat by beat

We Held On

When we started this love of ours, I feared losing you one day

Then I realized you were never mine to keep, wild and free

You are your own person, not an object to be possessed by anyone

When we fell in love with each other, there were emotions I had never felt

There was power in the love we shared to turn darkness into light

You changed me, and I will be forever grateful for the lessons in love you taught

When there were times I didn't understand love's ebbs and flows, there you were

I knew I had found the one person I wanted in my life until the end

We have never drifted entirely apart, even when there were times we wondered

When we have felt pain in our love, you were always the strength needed, holding on

I never knew there was a chance to hold someone like you in my arms

To look into your eyes until you turned away from me, the intense feeling we felt

When you told me of walls surrounding your heart, I wanted to rise above them

Just to get a glimpse into the heart of pure love, even after so much pain

I finally understand that there is someone like you, someone I could love back

When we struggled to understand the depth of a love like ours, we held on

Maybe longer than we should have, but now I want to say thank you for it all

I would take you into my arms again, to see the purity of the love we shared

Musings by M

Often, there comes a time when things seem to end. People drift apart and eventually, nothing is left. We will hold on and work to repair the issues; sometimes there are simple misunderstandings, sometimes there are significant issues. Time changes us all, and the change is so much of a difference that nothing can or will be done. We begin to look for something different for ourselves: a job, things, people. Other times, we can see the healing within the situation and work to repair the situation. Look for the lessons in every situation. There are times when there is a healing from it all. M

You Are a Miracle Amongst Us

Fighting every day to make sense of the life that has been handed to you

Yet every day, to face the challenges one by one, never backing down

A life that is never easy, you have conquered much, facing it all

They have tried time and time again to defeat you, only to retreat in defeat

Never conquering your strength, never taking your spirit from you

You have had armies arrayed against you, though bloodied, you have vanquished

A life filled with battles every day, waged to survive, you have never lost your courage

Disheartened at times, wanting it all to end, yet never backing down from each challenge

To be the person you are, despite the fights you have had, just to meet another day

You are a miracle amongst us, an angel sent to show the way, to love and cherish each of us

You have never had a life that has known peace within your heart and mind, a warrior to the end

You will one day leave this place and take with you the scars of every battle waged against you

Though so many have tried to destroy you, they have never known the power you hold within

As if an army of angels surrounds you and defends you to the last, your enemies will never win

Stand strong, you will end victorious, a warrior angel sent from above to end the hate arrayed against you

Musings by M

Some angels walk among us, sent to fight the battles we will never see. Some come to us in human form and face each day, lighting the way for us to know we, too, can face each of our enemies. They fight their past, they fight their demons, they fight the pain and sorrow heaped upon them by others. Some from childhood, some from those they thought they could trust. Reader and friend, understand that we all go through these battles, and know that you are a miracle among us. M

Once Within a Dream, I Saw

O nce, within a dream, I saw the love of one so fair

It was you, alighting upon a white steed, slowly moving towards me

I looked upon your radiance and knew I was seeing an angel from above

Once, within a dream, I saw a darkness, frightful and majestic

It was one, alighting upon a black steed moving slowly towards me

I looked upon the image and feared I would not survive an encounter

Once, within a dream, I saw the clarity of all my thoughts

It was me, alighting upon a steed, strong yet wild, refusing to be tamed

I looked upon the sights before me; memories came flooding into me

Once, within a dream, I saw the suffering of so many

It was an image of the pain the loveless have endured for so long

Broken, I collapsed to the ground beneath me, afraid to see more

Once, within a dream, I saw the world as it once was to be

Filled with joy, not knowing sorrow, filled with hope, not despair

I held my heart within my hand, broken yet still beating

Once, within a dream, I saw the laughter of the little ones

It was an image of a future yet to come, where joyous laughter filled the air

A sight to see, as they ran free, every color adorned them, as laughter filled the air

Once, within a dream, I saw more than I could comprehend

It saw a herd of wild horses, as the world alighted upon them all

As they carried each to the place they are meant to be, a life that belongs to all

Musings by M

Once, within a dream, came from somewhere other than me. As if it were handed to me by someone else. I am unsure I captured the essence of all that came to me, but I hope you understand its meaning. M

A Warrior's Prose to Love

Since I met you, beautiful, life has changed for me. I have understood what true love can be for the first time in my life. I am no longer holding back the love that has been simmering deep within me for so long. I have found the courage to face my demons head-on and defeat them. I have found my voice and am sharing my thoughts and emotions with the world. Your light, a torch of power, has given me that.

Our relationship has been fraught with many challenges but has remained strong in the face of so much pain and sorrow. You have given me your heart to hold and to cherish. I have given you my heart to guard. With all the attacks and all the hate, we have remained close and loving towards one another.

We have defended each other, sometimes causing each to doubt the truth of who we are, and yet, here we stand, united in this life we share. Your love for me strengthens me beyond measure. I hope beyond hope you know how much I genuinely love you.

The changes were needed for me to write again, and even though we have never had a life that has known peace, we have always conquered the evil around us. You do not know the power you hold within. So many have tried to destroy you and us but have failed. Your heart is pure, and your love runs deeply within the contours of your heart.

Your beauty goes beyond what people see. Exotic and mysterious as you are. Your true beauty is within. You deeply love those you choose to allow into your life. Friends, family, and thankfully, this weirdo.

Through these past years, you have been the one I could turn to when I felt overwhelmed by life. You have calmed my rage against all those who have tried to destroy you. You have given me a life I never want to lose. One of deep emotions and caring. If I have hurt you, in any way, I ask your forgiveness. I have never intended to cause hurt within you.

I have stood by you through all we have been through. I have tried to show you unconditional love. A love you deserve and will always be yours. Time and again, I ponder what our life would be like if there were peace around us, but I know we thrive in chaos. I look to a day when we face each day with renewed hope of a tranquility we have never known.

Forged in fire, our love grew from the flames of hate that encircled us, emerging stronger each time. Vanquishing those that are hell bent on destroying who we are together, a force the world has never known. Steadfast within this love, at times it has weakened, but never broken. Those who oppose our love, enraged by our love, will never understand. The depth of our love holds us true to each other.

We have only known battles and warfare against this love we share. Many have tried, all have failed to come between us. They will never break the bond we share; our love is stronger than any weapon used against us. A love forged in the fires of hate lit by those who desire to see us fall. Time will tell, stories will be written of our love through the ages. My warrior woman, may this warrior bard always stand beside you as we face the battles still to come, fighting for this love we share.

As we stand, facing each day with sword and shield in hand, defending our love in the face of so much hate, a pair the world will never conquer, our love will never cease to enrage our enemies, those hellbent on our destruction. For they know only hate for ones such as us, willing to fight for love. A love to last the ages, brought together by powers unseen, we stand, as one, to fight with those before us, willing to die for this love if we must. Bruised, battered, scared, and marked by the weapons of hate arrayed against us, yet here we stand, united in this love we share.

May we never weaken, may our love strengthen us as we face the daily battles against our love. May we always stand side by side, giving strength to each other. May our bond of love forever be strong.

Your warrior bard

Throughout history, there have been those who loved so deeply it seemed it would never end. There are stories of nations fighting for a love like this. A love that is willing to sacrifice itself for itself, to stand for a moment with the ones in love. Deep and sacrificial, never breaking. A love like this is rare to find, harder to live without. M

Earthly Angel

I can remember lying on my back, on a summer night, looking at the stars

Wondering what if they were angels sent to watch over each of us

What if they would one day fall from that sky and walk into my life

When you entered my life, you changed me; I became a better person with you

Never again looking back on the things I had done, but searching forward again

My life, the one I knew before you, became just a memory of the hurt and pain

Now that you have stayed in my life, I know that you are one of those angelic stars

Sent here to help me understand who I was meant to be, not who I was before

Having you stand with me, sheltering me from life's storms, protecting me from harm

I will do everything I can to help you understand how important you have become to me

You are my earth angel, sent from the sky above, healing my brokenness and fractured soul

You found me at my lowest and showed me there was hope to reach my highest

Thinking back on those summer nights, lying in the grass, and looking up at the stars

Did you see me then and knew one day we would be standing together, facing my fears

Were you sent to me to show me the way to a better life, my earth angel

Musings by M

Lying on the grass, looking to the sky. Have any of you thought about those stars? Is a falling star an angel falling to earth to walk with us? This is written to say that anyone in our lives could be our Earth Angel. Someone who came into our lives to help us. To walk with us for a season or the rest of our lives. M

Chapter Eight

A Chapter was Slammed on my Life

How do you replace part of your soul when that part is torn away?

How do you repair it when nothing that was torn away is left?

Nothing will be the same now that you are gone, such a waste

Taken from us far too fast, far too early for us to know and prepare

My soul is torn, damaged beyond repair, flapping in the storm

A chapter was slammed on my life, it isn't fair, it isn't right

The hurt, the anger, the pain, the loss will linger on

Musings by M

Dedicated to someone who loved a girl and protected her from abuse, a lifelong friend who was taken far too soon. M

Darkness Around

The thoughts of today are thoughts better left alone

With feelings coming to the surface of a life once lived

I wonder why this is so today, with the sun shining bright

There is only darkness all around me; I cannot see my way

So cold within my heart, yet trying to feel again, any feeling

I wonder why this is today, with so much warmth is finally here

There is a heaviness that has settled onto me, hard to even move

Like the weight of the world had control over me, my mind is clouded, too

Nothing seems to be clear to me; it is the darkness that controls me

Under this weight, my breath is labored and raging, fighting for the next one

The heart is still beating, but my mind has lost the desire to go on within darkness

What has become of me? I have no place to go, but I move through the day

Today, like every day, I try to make sense of all that is fighting against me

The darkness is stronger than the light I am seeking; I wander aimlessly

No direction, just knowing I need to try and move from here to there, I'm stuck

Darkness all around me, no light can be seen, I know there should be more

I struggle to make sense of the future for me, for my life, it feels so empty

Nothing seen, no one feels near, alone in the darkness of the day again

Musings by M

I felt the urge to write this today. I know this is a day of renewal and hope for many of you, but I don't know if this is for me or someone else today. Darkness, depression, and anxiety are weighing us down. I am okay, so don't worry about me. I hope the one or the others I wrote this for can make it another day. There is always hope, even when we don't see it right now. Don't give up, we can all move forward, even just one step at a time. M

From the Ashes

The strongest amongst us can one day be the weakest

When we have only known the need to be strong

There will come a day when life will one day bring us down

To the point of no longer wanting to fight for ourselves or others

Weakness is a struggle to overcome, and it makes us stronger in the struggle

When life no longer makes sense except for our will to survive, it

When time stands still for those who want to overcome the despair

They seek understanding in their struggles, fighting to regain strength

Out of weakness, there emerges a power many have never known

A power that is learned, a power that has come through during struggles

When there seemed no way out for them, they win the battle through all

Because for them, the only way out is through the narrow pass of understanding

When we can take our weaknesses and turn them into strengths, we change

We understand what weakness is; we see the struggles we had to go through

We know now that we can defeat our weaknesses and create our strengths

Out of the ashes of our struggles. We can finally see hope for a future for us.

There will come a day in every warrior's life when they experience weakness and despair. When all they have fought for seems hopeless. In these times, they look around at those they fought for and realize they are needed. They build up the strength to face another day and again enter the battle. M

Hurting Now

Hurting right now, a pain that is so overwhelming that you want to quit

The fighting, the struggling, the exhaustion of it all, feeling like you are done

You feel the pain as you try and get through each day, only the kids get you through

Not wanting to leave them, because of your love for them, keeps you moving

With all the loss you had to go through, with all the abuse you were forced to endure

It is beginning to come back and add to all you are going through now, exhausting

There seems there is nowhere to turn to escape this; it is in front of you all day long

Everyone feels untrustworthy, everyone seems to be against you, and you feel so alone

Abandoned by those you once trusted, it now seems they are all attacking you, the gossip

Who can you trust with all this? It seems that you are the only one whom you can trust

But now you are doubting even if you can trust yourself, exhausted, unable to sleep, tired

It has become more than you can handle at times, like you should just give up the fight

Where do you turn to now? Who is still a true friend or family member to help you?

You are confused by the fear of not knowing who you can trust, who can you trust now

It feels like you will never dig out from under the mountain that has fallen onto you

What is best for you, who has never let you down, who has always been there for you

Questioning your own sanity, have you always been this lost regarding who to trust

Not only with information or things happening to you, but with your heart and your love

Those you once trusted have always let you down, abused and used you, never true

Now you feel so alone in all these struggles you are going through, no one to trust, alone

Musings by M

There comes a point in everyone's life when the garbage that others have piled on becomes too much to handle anymore. We reach a point where we can no longer bear the weight of it. We begin to doubt others and ourselves. Due to the presence of jealous people around us, backstabbers, or even family and friends, we feel that we can no longer trust them with our thoughts or frustrations. Those we have confided in start spreading our conversations to others. We need to trust our friends and family to keep our discussions confidential. When that trust is broken, we even begin to doubt ourselves. The hurt this causes is a betrayal, and we lose the ability to speak our minds to others we once trusted. It is a hurt that leaves a scar on our hearts and minds. M

I am Without You

Far from what I wanted for us is what has happened

With everything we have been through together

The hate from people who don't like us together

The gossip from those who think they know why we are together

The time constraints kept us apart from one another

It felt like young love, that first real crush and relationship

There was magic, there is passion, there was power within us

Something was lost along the way; the magic went a different way

The power was lost, and the hot passion was reduced to cold indifference

You moved away from us, you moved away from me

Distance had grown so far away; it became too much to change

As I watched you walk away, my heart broke, and tears began to flow

My days are dark, my nights have grown cold, now that I am without you

Musings by M

When love ends between two people who once shared so much, it tears hearts apart with the loss. Never to be the same. Life changes, and loneliness sets in. Nights become the time when there is no hiding from the pain. M

Loving You Still

I have never forgotten the way you made me feel

From the day we met, I knew we would last a lifetime

Our love, our life together, would never be easy

But I knew it would be worth all the ups and downs

We have faced our share of joy-filled times and sorrow

But it would make us stronger and more alive, in our love

We would face whatever life threw our way, together as one

Life will not be easy, but life lived with you is worth it

My life changed the day I met you; it changed and became amazing

Walking with you in my life has shown me who I really am and can be

I don't want another person walking with me, loving me, in my life

You have a way about you that has brought me peace that I never knew

Hearing your voice, looking into your beautiful eyes, still moves me

It is so wonderful knowing that you feel the same way for me as well

Knowing your love, even when times have gotten tough, we have each other

We have been through so much, but we are still together, love shared

Musings by M

Whether you are still with them or not, you cannot forget the way you feel for them the minute you first met them. They may have swept you off your feet from the beginning. When things get too much, think back on what drew you to them in the first place. It may be their looks, maybe the way they spoke, their personality, or all of it. During the struggles in your relationship, think back on that first meeting you shared.

You Question

You question everything about us. Are we supposed to be together or not

You're fearful of making a mistake when it comes to allowing yourself to love me

Never before have you been shown a love like the love I have for you

You question why I love you, though I have given you a thousand reasons why

You look at yourself and think there is nothing to love within you, I see it even so

You have been hurt so many times before, I am not like the others, my love is true

You question how I can love someone like you, wondering if I am just using you

I have stood by you in the good times we shared, and the brokenness of what you left me

Yet you still doubt if I am the one for you when others seemed to be the one before

You question if love will ever come your way, losing your love for me because of fear

I see an amazing person standing before me, you are perfect for me, even broken

There is no need to doubt how deeply I love you, I am yours to love or dispose of

You question me, looking for a reason to either love me or dispose of me this time

I show love that is unconditional, even when there are times you break my heart

My love for you is what I want to give you, even when you question my love for you

Musings by M

There is a point in every relationship when one or both begin to question the relationship. Those times can cause doubt and fear to seep into it. But if there is honest and open communication between both parties, there is also room for discussion. Sometimes one or both have not been in a healthy relationship. When that happens, and it does often, there is room for showing each other unconditional love. A love worth standing up for is rare anymore. Love openly and honestly, and when doubts do arise, love each other through them. M

Twisting and Turning

Twisting and turning is the road I am walking right now

I cannot see what is around the corner in front of me right now

No view of what to expect around the corner, I am approaching now

I encounter surprises around every corner as I turn to continue on my road

People and situations appear out of nowhere; it is so strange to me

As I deal with one thing, something different emerges as I move forward

I am struggling to make sense of everything I am facing; it has knocked me back

Why is my life full of so many barriers as I attempt to move forward? Every turn adds to it

There was a time when I knew where I was to go, now only confusion seems to haunt me

Where am I to go except to move forward, one step at a time, moving slowly but steadily

I must move forward, each step takes me to the finish line, will I ever get there

Who will be waiting for me when I finally get there? Who is waiting for me to reach the end?

Musing by M

Life seems to be twisting and turning me these days. Nothing is as it seems. Instead of seeing down the path I am on, there are blind corners everywhere I turn. I can no longer see too far in front of me. I am blind to my future. There is a sense of dread with every step I take. M

The Strewn Path

As we age, our bodies begin to break down, things that took a day to overcome seem to last

The pains we feel become more frequent and seem to last beyond what was normal

Life has a way of catching up to each of us, some things stay the same for some, though

Some have found a fountain of youth deep within them; they never seem to age like others

Others struggle just to get through another day to find a few hours rest and repose again

Some sit down and wait for the inevitable and await that final walk, being laid to rest

I am reminded that I am no longer the youth I was once; he is still there, but there is an old man here more

The pains of my youth seem to be knocking more on my door than I remember, a reminder of times gone by

There is less sleep and more thoughts of what is coming for me; seems these days, I am beginning to fail

I have never been the best of people, though I always tried to provide for those I have loved and cared about

I was never a perfect man, but I have tried to show the love I still feel in my heart for those I love. I hurt many

I have watched them grow, become people in their own right, and forge ahead, despite me and anything I have done

I am not asking forgiveness for the wrongs I have caused. As the years have passed, the pain has grown, even though I tried

Forgiveness comes from the heart, understanding comes from the mind, resolution comes between two to set things right

I know I have hurt others by words and deeds, which seemed right to me at the time, looking back on them, I see the errors I have made

One day I will leave this place, my time was set for me long ago, and I have defied death many times throughout my life, to what end I know not why

But as I look back across the path strewn with the brokenness I have left behind, I realize I was wrong and will have my eternity to contemplate it all

Some may mourn, some may celebrate, but in the end of all of this, please know my weak attempts to show love were all I had to give you all

Musings by M

This one is deep. Written on a bitterly cold day. Clouds obscure the sun, and still, traces of snow are coming down. Allow this Musing to sink in and let it heal what can be healed. M

As I Reflect

As I reflect on my life today, there is so much to see for me

I sit here and wonder what happened to the life I once wanted

There is not much left of the person I used to be; much is lost

As I reflect on the places I have been, physical as well as mentally

I have not reached those places; I have been close but never there

I wonder if things were different, what would be that reflection I would see

As I reflect about those I have had enter my life, where are they all now

Would I feel so alone even with them here with me, am I the same I used to be

When will there be those who I thought I needed, they seem to have left me to me

As I reflect on the love I have felt for family and for friend, was it a waste for me

Walking alone in this life, now that they have all seemed to have abandoned love

The path I am on is it for me alone, or am I to have someone to love me along the way

As I reflect on the past, I see so many leaving me, was it me or them that walked away

When did I lose so much? was it to teach me, or to show me that it was never meant to be

I have walked through so many storms; I have almost lost my way through them all

As I reflect on another year of my survival, so much has changed within me

A teaching year, I must have needed to understand the life I am to have

A reflection of the times to come; within the sadness, there, it is filled with hope

Musings by M

Self-reflection of what has been. Looking back to see the path walked upon. Where are those who once meant so much to one such as I, we might think. Life, with its wins and losses, ever changing us into people we were meant to become. How do we self-reflect and yet face each day with renewed hope? Time will tell, for each of us. M

Encircled

Encircled within the thoughts from my past, the good and the bad

Whirling around within my mind, showing me my mistakes, I have made

Some were small and easy to fix, some were big and painful to see again

Encircled within my fears, will I ever know peace in my mind and my soul

Seeing those I have hurt with my words and my actions, never far away

I know I have hurt those I should have cared about, those who cared for me

Encircled within my memories, some are still good to see, others bring so much pain

Beating myself up for the hurts I have given to others and to myself

Looking into my memories, I see the tears that I have cried over the things I have done

Encircled by feelings I still hold for some that have walked out of my life, never to return

The emotions those feelings bring to me can break my heart once again

Feelings of feeling alone, feelings of loss of those who meant so much to me

Encircled by my past, fighting all of those feelings and memories, hurt as they swing at me

I do my best to defend myself, but I am encircled by all of them at once

Fighting for peace, fighting for forgiveness of myself, when no one has given it to me

Musings by M

Life can encircle us as we deal with it, both the good and the bad of life. Sometimes we feel like we are fighting in the round, all around us are issues, problems, our past, and our present. People seem to want us to fail. They strike at us to hurt us. Sometimes someone comes along to help, but can just as quickly disappear. The times we feel like we are fighting all alone, it can seem horribly overwhelming. All we can do is fight on and hope to conquer. M

The Past

The past came back to me again, telling me to give up, I am, I am worthless

Always there, just a word or thought away, always there haunting me

Why won't it let me go, so I can move on from it, still just there waiting

Trying to remind me of all the mistakes I have made, I can't escape it

The memories of my failures haunt me, those I hurt. Those who walked away

The anger begins again to build within me; the past begins to laugh at me

Telling me I will never get away from my past because of all I have done

I cannot turn left or right, move ahead, or turn back; it is always there, taunting

All I want is peace in my heart and mind, knowing I will get past what I did before

I want to be a different person, but my past yells at me that I am still the same

How do I change myself to become the one I want to be when the past is always there?

Is there no hope for me of changing and becoming someone new and different

My past, sitting there watching my every move, stopping me from making changes

I slip back into my old ways and want to give up on becoming a better person

When I reach for help, my past tears my arm away, forcing me to remain stuck again

What can I do to change my future when the only thing I see is the past that still haunts me?

Musings by M

Our past can control our future if we allow it to do so. We all have a past. We have all done things we wish we hadn't done, but we did. Instead of stopping us, we can all change. Some will need help, some can change by sheer will. M

A Clown

There are times when I feel like I am just the village idiot

Everyone seems to smile at me, but hold some fear of me

No one stands with me as I speak the words I need to say

Instead, behind closed doors, they mock me and laugh at me

There are times I feel like a clown in a small circus, face paint hiding me

I long to feel alive again, but instead, I hide in my sorrows

No one seems to care if I'm ready to burn it all down anymore

Why do I give myself the pain of trying to hold on to any hope now

There are times I feel like I am just a jester who is trying to make others smile

While I fight back the tears and the hate I feel every time I look in the mirror

Never liked that person, seems no one else does, what's the point anymore

I am not what people think I am, I hurt more than feel peace and joy in my life

There are times when I know I have failed so many in my weak attempts to hold on

I have driven more away from me than ever brought to me

I am wrong more than I am right, I have hurt them more than helped them

I am not the person people see me as; I am far less than they really know

There will come a day when I will be gone from the lives of all of you

I don't even know six people who would be willing to carry me to my final place

I have isolated myself from the pain by isolating myself from the world around me

Never belonging in this place, I finally know that and I am just a clown to you all

Musings by M

We have all felt unwanted at times. There are moments when we feel the pain from deep within, of not being loved the way we feel we deserve. There have been times in my life when I felt so down, so unloved and unlovable that I didn't even like myself. This was written as a means to carry myself and others through those times. Since we have all experienced moments of self-doubt, we often think we are not loved. Love will find a way to heal our brokenness and take the pain from our hearts, trust in love. M

Life is a Series

L ife is a series of ups and downs for most everyone, I
  think

Life can be good at times, and life can be bad at times for
all of us

It is how we deal with all of it that makes us who we are

During the bad times, we can wallow in the pain of them,
feeling lost

Yet by looking for the lesson, we can grow stronger,
willing to face the next

If we only bemoan the bad, we can get stuck in an endless
cycle of bad

During the good times, we can think they will never leave us, joyous about the good

If we are truly thankful for the good, we can also learn a lesson from these times

We will understand better why we enter good times when the bad come back again

Life is a series of good and bad, high and low, togetherness and separation

We are given time to learn and to help us grow, to become stronger and more alive

To understand the differences of each and embrace the lessons taught in both

Musings by M

Life, in general, is a series of highs and lows. When we are up, we get excited, and it seems like life is ours to enjoy. When the lows hit us, we become worried and sad because life is not what we had when things were going well. Life is a time to learn lessons. What are the lessons in both of these times? M

They Tried to Destroy You

They have tried to destroy you, but it is like they broke a mirror

Seven years of bad luck each time they have tried to break you

Baby, you are blessed with a way to survive all they throw at you

They continue to do what they can to bring you down, never able to

Others have tried, but they are cursed by the effort to harm you

Protected by those who led you to where you are now, they lost

They will never learn who you really are and how protected you are from harm

They try and try and never succeed, failing every time they try to hurt you

There are forces against them, even though they are too blind to see

They will lose interest one day, and they will remember who you are

It will be too late for them, but they can warn the next group who will try

You are blessed, baby, with protection against those who want to harm you

Stronger than they know, more powerful than all your enemies

One day, they will stop, and you will know what peace really feels like

Until that day, they will continue to try and will fail every time

Hold your head high as you walk through the storms they try to bring against you

You are shielded from the fury of each and every storm life throws at you

They will finally learn you are an angel sent from above to fight them all

Musings by M

Many people fight every day to make it to the next day. They are targeted by people who are jealous and hate-filled. If you know one of these angels in human form, stand with them and they will bless you beyond anything you have imagined. Their strength, their courage, their love for others, even in the face of all hate, will help you become the person you are meant to be. M

My Battles

M y battles are not with anyone else; they are all within my heart and mind

I fight to continue to face every day with hope, when I just want to give up

I struggle to make sense of the way the world has changed around me

My fight to keep my head up when I feel like just walking away and disappearing

I have struggled so long with self-doubt and self-loathing due to my pain and sorrow

I am tired of the war I have been fighting against myself and others, almost my whole life

I need time away where nothing can hurt me again, where my heart can heal and my mind rest

Where healing myself is the priority, and the rest of it can be put aside for a time

I have no idea when that will be, but I know it will be one day, a time for just myself

My battles have been waged, my war is deep within, I have fought the good fight, bloody and battered

Yet there has to be a time in my life where I can finally find peace, when the war has ended, and I find rest

I am not sure if that will ever happen for me, but I long to walk away from all of this. I am tired of my battles

Please understand it is not all who I have known who have caused me this pain, some have tried to love me too

This is my war, fought more with myself than with others, where I can never seem to win, but I will fight on

I hope one day to be the victor and no longer the victim of my self-hate and self-loathing

Musings by M

There was a time in my life, and I am sure in many others' lives, where this musing is true. When we fight to make sense of the life we are fighting to change, and how hard it is to overcome our past and all the things we have been through. Some at our own hand, some because of others. Yet, we fight to be better at times, wanting to give up, but we approach each day, fighting to change our future. May the battles within each of us not be to win, and may each tomorrow be a step towards a better tomorrow. M

A Dream

I once had a dream that I wasn't me and that this wasn't my life

No one used me to become someone else, as they pushed me away again

There was a smile on the face of the person who I saw in my dream, a happy person

I woke up and ran to the mirror, hoping to find that person standing in front of me

But when I looked, I realized it was only me staring back; tears began to fall

I went back to my bed and fell back to sleep, hoping to find that person again

As I slept, I had another dream, one where I was the center of my own life, but not alone

Where people would say they were happy to see me and tell me they loved me

I smiled in that dream, I felt alive and loved for the first time in my life, I was wanted

In the morning, I went to look in the mirror again and I realized it for the first time in my life

I could be the love to others that I sought to find in someone else, not alone anymore

You are the person I have been searching for I said to the person in the mirror

When we love ourselves and understand who we are to us, the love we seek will come to us

We will find the love we seek by showing love to others they will be drawn to our light of love

Always find your inner peace, and the world will see the love you have to share with others

Musings by M

There comes a time in all our lives when
we realize we need to find ourselves as we
are. We should be good in our own skin and
stop trying to be someone else. When we do,
others will show us who we are. M

Just Once

Just once, I want to have all my dreams be realized instead of this

Dreams shattered all the time, never getting what I desire just once

My life is not the life I wanted, sitting here alone and broken

This bottle in my hand ain't healing the brokenness I feel inside

Just once, I want things to happen for me, not to me anymore

I have been pushed away by so many; I am battered and torn

Life for me is hate, not love, and it tears me apart every day

All I wanted was to find peace, but what I find is war within my heart

Just once, I want to know what it is that has led me down this road

Why is there nothing and no one for me to turn to? I am so alone

What did I do to deserve all of this? This bottle is my only friend

And I hate the way it makes me feel, so empty and so damned alone

Just once, I want to feel alive again and not have to numb the pain I find

Only breathing and fighting the urge to end it all, now what am I left to feel

Was I cursed the day I was born, because it sure feels like I was from the beginning

Struggled my whole life to make sense of all the hate I have been shown

Just once, I want to look in the mirror and love the one I see there inside

But I turn the light off and only see the demons standing behind me

Never a moment of peace do I feel, as I reach for the only friend I have left

I lift it to my lips and take more in to numb the pain I feel so deep inside of me

Musings by M

This was written after I listened to a song, and it struck me that so many are hurting and fighting to take one more step. They have fought their past for so long that they believe the only recourse is to numb the pain. Addictions of any type can be the hardest thing to fight. Feeling hopeless and helpless, they only find comfort in their addiction and numb the pain. Those who have been able to break the cycle are the strongest people I have ever met. I am proud to know each of you. M

Valley of Darkness

M ost of my life, I have felt like I was walking through a valley

Not one I would choose for anyone, it is a valley of darkness

Nothing can be seen but hopelessness and sorrow all around

I have faced loss and loneliness more than hope and love

It never seems to get better for me. I have stumbled and crawled

When there was even a hint of hope, it was torn away again from me

I have tried to continue to move forward, searching for something better

Each time I thought I found it, Something tore it away again from me

Left with nothing to hold onto, again, alone in my despair

Until I find the opening that will allow the light to shine on me again

I must fight my way through this valley of darkness alone to reach the other side

I will never give up on the hope of finding my way through the darkness, crawling if I must

Even when despair and hopelessness are all around, I want to just give up on it all

I will move forward, even if it is just an inch a day, until I reach the light once more

I cannot wallow in this darkness forever; it will destroy me one day, so I must move on

Through the pain I feel deep within me and all the suffering and sorrow, I must move on.

I will get lost, and I will have to start again, I will fall, and have to rise again, it is never easy

But I must move, though at times the weight of all this sorrow seems to overwhelm me

Through a valley of darkness, the jeering and lies heard all around me must never end me

I am stronger than the constant trials I face, and I search for light in this darkness; there must be hope

If I never try to leave this place, I will die broken and alone, within this valley of darkness

Musings by M

So many fight every day with addictions and mental health issues, it feels like they are in the darkness. They fight and struggle to survive, searching for a light to guide them through the darkness and back into the light. We all face our own valley of darkness at some point. What yours is will be different from mine. Most can make it through the hopelessness and pain, but some never will. M

No Longer Your Hero

When did you change the way you see me, no longer your hero

I am not sure what I did to make you change the way you see me

Was it yesterday, or did it change long ago for you towards me

When did I lose your love for me? What did I do that changed your feelings

What is the cause for the change? Is it me or is it you that has changed

I have only wanted you to be the person you were to be my child

I know I can be difficult to understand, I am not easy to understand most days

So much of me is difficult to love as well, as I am not like most parents of adult kids

Once I was the one you would come to for help with hurts, now I am the last for you

Why has this all changed what did I do to incur your wrath and your dismissal of me

Anger and hurt is what you told me you feel towards me now, I will step away now

I will be willing to talk when you are ready, but I will not beg for you for love again

I didn't realize I did anything other than be me, I am no longer enough for you, it's clear

All I can do is allow you to sort through your thoughts and feelings of things now

If you call me parent again, that is for you to decide. I will never force you to love me

This is written from the perspective of a parent to a child, but it spans the entirety of life and love, encompassing families, relationships, and even deep-rooted friendships. Interchange words to fit your situation. Hope it helps everyone make sense of life and love. M

A Series of Highs and Lows

Life has become a series of highs and lows for me anymore

There seems to be far more lows than highs though

Never making sense of all I am going through, yet trying to understand

When I think of each of you, I wonder if any of you understand the strain

With my mind full of memories of times spent with those I love and cherish

Now it seems as if I have not really lived them, but are only dreams

I have always tried to be the best I could be for those that I love

Yet it seems that life has chosen me to struggle to understand

I long for happier times spent with those I have known and love still

Even as my days and nights run together, there is a flurry of activities I never making it through

I enter a quiet and dark building where I lay my head and try to sleep away the pain

Awakening to another sunrise, feeling as if rest will never come to my mind

Time and time again, I face the world with the mask I know you want me to wear

It is so you will not see the sorrow in my eyes as I greet another day in this world.

I fear if you knew the struggles deep within you would turn from me and walk away.

Fighting every waking hour to turn the tide on my pain and sorrow, losing more than I win

The weight of all that faces me is more than I can bear to lift every single day of this life.

I chose not to give up, but there are times when I so badly want to just stop the fight

Musings by M

Life is never easy, but for those fighting depression or other mental health issues, it is an even bigger battle every day to make it through. Many fight hard to overcome it, and some never do. We all experience highs and lows in life, and it often seems like we want to give up fighting and surrender to the darkness we feel inside. Never give up, please know some walk with you every day through the struggles. M

You Drew Away

Y ou drew away from me, and I just thought it was because you needed space

Here I stand, wondering if it was a sign that things had ended between us that day

Yet we are close and in love still, but something has changed between us now

You drew away, saying that things were not the same, that we needed to spend time apart

That one-day things would make sense to me, and I would understand, yet I am more confused

When did things become the way they are for us now? Was it the time you drew away from me

You drew away from me as I was reaching for you again, as if it hurt you to feel me close

The love we have shared was so powerful to me that I knew life would never be the same for me

Yet you stood before me and seemed to put a distance I didn't want between us

You drew away from everything yet told me that one day we would be together again

Life has never been the same for me since that day feeling so alone and longing for your touch

When will you give to us again what happened to cause you to distance yourself from me?

You drew away from me and from our life, changing everything in my life that day

Love, I feel still within my heart, still stirs my world to seek to feel you close to me again

My heart has never given up on us, as I love you as much today and when we were as one

When the one we love draws away from us, it can be a confusing and painful experience. We long to understand the reasons why. Life seems to change around us, and we try to make sense of the new world we've been thrust into. When love ends for one, does it end for both? When love ends for one, does it end for both? Some would say yes, others would say no. M

Nothing Makes Sense

When nothing makes sense to us, the why of it all is lost to all of us

There are times we feel so lost in a world that doesn't understand who we are

We are all a wreck most days as we walk around people who don't see into our hearts

We want everyone to know that we want them all to feel better, loved, and appreciated

That they can understand their value to those who love them, no matter the past

There is more to life than the hate held in their broken hearts, because life let them down

Many of us have never known love, those we once loved never loved us truthfully

They used us and then abandoned us when we were no longer useful or wanted by them

Thrown away to pick up the pieces lying in a wake of fakeness, never real, never honest

Living life in the shadows of the pain and heartbreak we have been through is so cold

Afraid of being hurt again, but longing for someone real to love us even in our brokenness

Not judging us for our past but for who we really are deep inside, someone to see our light

We all want a love that will walk with us through all the troubles and storms that life throws at us

Someone who will hold us tightly, as we shield each other from all the pain of life

Who will stand by us, and love us with a true and honest love, a love to last the test of time

A love that doesn't set conditions, a love that will never break, even when it is hard to love us some days

Someone who will not abandon us, like everyone else has before, a love to last a lifetime, healing, and bold

We just need to know we have value when everyone has shown us we are not worthy of love or hope

Musings by M

There are people walking around us every day who have never known unconditional love from anyone. They were raised by people who imposed conditions on the love they received. They move through life believing they have to earn the love of another. Then one day, someone enters their life and changes that. The love that is offered does not come with a price tag attached. If you have never been loved unconditionally, it will take time to understand that there are no conditions on the love they receive and give. M

Fighting for Another Day

Life has become a series of fate-filled chances to get it right

As I look back on this thing I have walked through called life, I wonder

If it should have belonged to someone else, or was it meant for me

What has become of all the hopes and dreams I once had

Life has become more like episodes of a tragic comedy than a life

Where things and people have been taken or destroyed, but life itself

So much has happened through the years to me and to others around

Why must it always be a battle to survive instead of a life to live in peace

Life, at least my life, has not been what I dreamed of as a child

Instead, it has been filled to hopelessness and sorrow, not what I hoped for

The tragedy of it all is that much has been caused by the choices I have made

There is brokenness and pain left behind as I have tried to do what I thought was right

Life for me has had its ups and downs, it has seemed for me it was more down than up

Never having what I thought I wanted, but surviving to face another day

I don't wish my life on anyone to have to walk the path I have chosen; it saddens me now

Why has it been this way for me? What was the cause of all the loss and sorrow I have faced

Life, it seems funny now, the word itself denotes something alive and growing each day

Yet here I sit, in the shadow of the past, as I look back on all I have been through

Many would not believe the way each breath has changed me, each day has been tough

Yet as I awaken each day to face another day of this life, I know my time is growing shorter

Life, my life, is not the one I had hopes and dreams of as a child; this is not what I wanted

It seems it has been given to me to struggle through and to look back on with sorrow

I have lost many, I have suffered and struggled to make it to the next day far too often

Yet it is the hand that I was dealt so long ago, never gaining but always fighting for another day

Musings by M

Broken Now

R ising from my bed, I realize you will never be here
with me; you are gone

Never going to be able to see you again because I can't
see you now

Why did you have to leave me here and never be able to
be together again

I went to pour a cup of coffee, and I felt a tear roll down
my face. I am alone

We used to sit together and drink our coffee on days just
like today

When it was cold outside, we would sit together and hold
each other

I sit here, and I can feel the rage boiling up inside, knowing you are gone now

We will never be able to talk about our dreams again, you are not coming back

Lost to me, I am alone, lost in my thoughts, rage turns to sorrow; I am alone

Why did you get taken from me? What am I supposed to do now without you?

We had so many dreams of our tomorrows, but they are all broken now

Alone here now, I hear the birds singing their songs outside the window, forlorn songs

I feel cold and alone, lost in the memories of our days together, they are now gone

What is left to me without you here with me? How am I to go on living a life alone

I want you back, but I have to face my days alone; you are not coming home to me

You are the love of my life, the one I knew would always be here for me to hold me tight

Now you are gone from me, and you will never come home to me again. I am now alone

Life is never fair, love can break a heart, when you love someone so much, and now they are gone

Musings by M

The loss of love for any reason can leave a person feeling drained of hope. When a marriage of love ends, one is left picking up the pieces, some never more beyond the brokenness and loss. When it is due to the passing of someone, it can shatter all dreams and hopes in the one who is left behind. Memories of daily activities can trigger emotions to flood back into the minds of those left behind. Most recover enough to move on with their lives, but some never will. M

Chapter Nine

When I Think of You

When I think of you I find myself wandering through so many thoughts

They come in waves when you are not here beside me, loving you deeply

I find the thoughts of holding you and looking into your eyes so filled with love

When I think of you, I want you here by my side never leaving me again

I can listen to you speak of the future we share and all the love you have for me

Knowing you has changed my life for all the right things never wanting another

When I think of my life before you entered it, what was happening to me was empty

Never have I felt the way I do for you; we are meant to stand together until the end of time

Life has been so full and amazing since I met you, I am beginning to understand my past

When I think of the struggles I went through the loss and the heartache gave me a heart to love

You are the most amazing one, a person filled with love and hope of what life can be

Never have I met someone like you, even though you are scared to love me, I love you so

When I think of how you have changed so much about me, I am happy after so much sorrow

We were meant to form the bond we share this love to last the ages, finally finding peace

Our life will never be the same, we have found the one to heal our hearts and souls

Life can take us and change us from who we thought we were. It can change what we thought we were or thought what we were to do. Changing the one we are to love unexpectedly. Someone enters our life and loves us in so many amazing way than we thought we deserved. It is amazing to us, life can now finally make sense. M

I Think Of

I think of you, and I know that my love for you has never changed

But I wonder if you love me the way I love you still, or have you changed

So many secrets and time away from each other is hard on this love I have for you

I think of our love and long to hold you in my arms right now, to feel you close

But there is distance between us at the moment, it seems I may have lost you

What am I to think when you stay so busy with other things there is no time for us

I think of the times we have shared so much it seems you have distanced yourself from me

What am I to think when I long for you so much and yet you seem so far away from me now

Will you tell me what is causing this or leave it up to me to decide the course I must take

I think and at times I over think this situation right now, what do you honestly feel for me

You tell me you love me still, but I wonder if that is from habit or true feelings you have

I ask for you to tell me, yet you seem to do everything you can not to say what is going on

I think you have lost love for me, but you tell me I worry too much about things right now

You are trying to work more to make ends meet, but I am always here for you to help

Come to me and openly tell me why things have changed so much between us

Musings by M

Don't overthink every situation, because
we all can do that at times. When
patterns change, doubts can begin to grow.
Communicate with each other as to the why,
so the doubts can be minimized. Love might
conquer and understanding the situation
will be made clear. M

Cherish You

There is never a day I don't think about you my love

I hold you close to my heart daily and I love you so much

Today, like yesterday, as it will be tomorrow, I will love you always

Life can be strange, yet it is also so amazing, this love I have for you

This love I feel for you will never change for me, you are so amazing to me

But you never see how amazing you truly are, a person who has so much love

I am honored to call you my love, the love of a lifetime for me

You have changed me so much and yet you still don't understand me

This love I feel for you has been the strength that has changed me, and I thank you

Our love has given me the courage to change my path in life, it has been so amazing

A day with you feels like a minute for me, but you still don't understand

That life for me was so dark and empty until you entered my life, I was so alone before

Never will I look back to the life I knew before, life has opened up to me

I will never go back to the life I once knew, a life now full of love and joy with you

Thank you for giving me your heart to have and to hold, I cherish you each day

Musings by M

When we begin to feel love for another person, life begins to become different. We no longer just think of ourselves but we think of the 2 involved, if the romance is blossoming. As time goes and feelings grow, life becomes sweeter and become more willing to think of a possible future with our person. Allowing for more thoughts of a future together. We should cherish every moment we get to spend with each other, one day there will not be another moment to share. M

Life Before You

All the struggles, the fighting myself to make sense of my life before you

All the frustrations and all the battles I fought to get here to you never made sense

Why did I have to go through everything I did before I met you almost destroyed me

All of it, all of the pain and the hurt I went through just to arrive to you were worth it

I understand now why it all had to happen to get me here to where you and I met

There were changes I needed to make to be able to love you the way you deserve

All the time I was being formed into someone who will take you to your fulness

When we met, the sparks were there never had I met someone like you

There was a feeling that we had met before, long ago and were meant to meet again

All the life I had lived and all I had lost cleared the path for me to finally find you

Together we are meant to face the world, side by side we will fight for the life we deserve

Without having to battle to make it to that day, I never would have been ready for this love

All the love we have shared has been something so sweet and so new to me, it shook me deeply

I have never met someone so amazing, so adorable, so deeply loving like you so perfect for me

A person who accepts me for me with all my flaws and weaknesses, yet loving me even so

All those years I felt alone and lost just wandering through life until you entered my life that day

I finally felt a love for someone who understands me who loves me the way you love me

We have been destined to find each other after so much pain and hurt, together we are made whole

Musings by M

Within all the struggles of life, heartache and pain are molding us. We are being prepared to finally find a life and love that will last. All the brokenness of life and love can be healed with the one we finally find that will love us and we can love them through the healing. One day, a person will enter our life and wipe away the past, offering a future to each other that will heal us. M

Not Like Others

From the day we met I never wanted to disappoint you about anything

I have always tried to do the things I told you I would do, never forgetting

Once I found you and we fell in love, we made a promise to always be there

You have been treated, by so many, as a plaything that you had no value

Once they were finished with you they would toss you away and find another

But I am not like the others, and I want to show you what love can really be

169

We have never had an easy tome within this love we have shared us

But I know our lives would be so empty without the other, here

We deserve to know what love can feel like and you have shown me your love

Never wanting to let you down, you do the same for me, we are here for each other

Our love is easy too, the feelings flow between us, and we enjoy our love we share

I want to show you that I love you because words can be just words without actions

We found each other when neither was looking for anyone to fall in love with

But now the love we share has changed us both, we have finally found a real love

We talk of a future together and are making plans to move our lives along each day

We never want to disappoint each other, we have finally found a love to last a lifetime

A love to weather the storms of life and a love that is easy to feel and enjoy together

We fell in love and made a promise to never let the other down, we know that pain from others

Musings by M

After a lifetime of disappointments, we become fearful of new love coming into our lives. We are guarded and wait for the repeating behaviors from before. But there is always someone who can help us heal from our past, showing us a love, we have never known, but always wanted. This person is not like others, they are the healing we have needed. M

So Amazing

Lost many things along the way to where I am today, most can be replaced

Friends have gone from me and others have taken their place in my life

But if I lost you, there is no way I could ever replace you, my world would end

When you entered my life you chased the sorrow and my past away from me

You offered me your hand and a love like I have never known, so amazing

Showing me that I could heal and learn to love and trust again after so long

I have never known someone like you, someone who gave light back to my life

Who taught me to understand that love can be found again in my heart

The one person who was able to thaw the frozenness deep within my heart

When you entered my life and loved with a love I never knew I would find

A love that changed me and showed me that I could love again and come alive

You offered me your hand and a love like I have never known you are amazing

Musings by M

So amazing, is a Musing that echoes what so many hearts long for when they are struggling through life. We have all lived periods that seemed we were lost and alone. Then one day someone enters our world and brings healing to our brokenness. Light to chase away the darkness we have stumbled through for so long. Life and love, embraced in a love like nothing we have ever known, love so amazing. M

Broken

Even in my brokenness, you saw me buried deep inside and loved me

Within your brokenness, I saw you hidden from even yourself and loved you

Our love has healed us both and the world was always so shocked we did

My healing started when you wrapped me in your arms and this love we share

I hope you know how much you have helped me to heal and change just being you

With your love, I have finally felt peace in every inch of me no longer just darkness

We have changed each other in ways neither of us knew was possible before

You were never loved completely and unconditionally, I never was either, always a catch

Someone people would use for their benefit and then abandon when we served our purpose

Our love has been the glue we needed to become whole again, this love has healed us both

The joys we share, the laughter and the love, is something we wanted but never found before

Thank you for showing me that I can be better than I thought I could be with your love

You saw my brokenness and understood the healing you could give me with just your love

I saw your brokenness and thought I could help you heal from everything you went through

Together we are helped each other become whole again and love each other through the process

Musings by M

So many are broken from their past. Broken by family, friends, or former loves. Then one day someone enters their life and finally love them truly, healing the brokenness caused by others. They help each other heal from the past. Have you found yours? M

You Are Meant for More

How can you not see the person you are to so many

After all these years of watching you and how amazing you really are

You still don't know that you are the most amazing person I have ever known

Time and time again, I explain why I adore you but you find it difficult to see

The person you are because of all the pain others caused you before me

They told you for so long you are worthless, but I know you are a rare gem

For so long others, because they feared you, convinced you that you have no value

Yet in the years I have known you, I know you are the one priceless person I've ever known

Someone who has a healing presence and a way of healing the broken around you, just not you

Because you have known so much pain and sorrow, you work to make others not feel the same

You go out of your way to help the helpless and broken, to heal them and pick up the pieces

Never have I met someone who could touch so many in a healing way like you do

Even as I tell you how beautiful you are, you try and change the subject, because you doubt it

Yet deep within your heart is so much love and care, it overflows wherever you go in life

Please understand that you are beyond amazing, you are beautiful and loving, you are meant for more

Musings by M

When we have lived in the darkness of others' opinions and thoughts of who they convince us we are, it can be difficult to understand who we truly are. We have so much to give to ourselves and others, but all we see is what they have told us we are. When we can finally break free of them, we can see ourselves, oftentimes for the first time. M

When You Look in the Mirror

When I met you the first thing I saw was what you look like

As I got to know you what I saw was what was inside you

Your heart, bigger than the sun glowing with a passion for life

When you look in the mirror then you saw a young vibrant one

No blemishes, nothing to make you worry about regarding aging

You still saw the flaws on you beautiful face, ones I still don't see

When you look in the mirror before, there was beautiful hair

Flowing as you combed it to get ready to leave and face the world

Now you see gray beginning to appear and the need to cover it

When you look in the mirror you saw curves, beauty in your eyes

The world told you how you should look a certain way to appeal to others

Now you see things filling out, imperfections on your body, and cringe

When I look at your face, I see the face of someone I love without fear

Beauty beyond what you believe, the face of the one I love

Beautiful and amazing, someone I am spending every day loving

When I look at your hair, I see the hair of the one I have loved for so long

The hair I love to feel against my skin as we embrace each other

The hair that frames the face I love to look at as you talk about your day

When I look at your body, I can see the one who has always drawn me in

The person I fell in love with, the one I have shared so much love with

Someone I long to hold in my arms, someone I am proud to show the world

When I look at you, I see the one person I want to stand by me all the rest of my days

The one I long to hold when you are not here with me, whose eyes sparkle with love

The one I never want to lose, the one I love beyond all others, the one I want by side

When I fell in love with you, I fell in love with all of you, the amazing one that you are

When I wake in the morning, with you by my side, I know life is beautiful and worth living

When I hear that soft morning spoken in sleepiness, I know love for one like you

Musings by M

Men and women age, but society has placed more value on the outside appearance of each of us, instead of what is important, the beauty of a person's heart and soul. Outward beauty fades naturally for us all, inner beauty lasts until the end. We should look beyond what we see with our eyes and feel the inner beauty of the one we fell in love with and cherish still. M

Life of Love

You came to me when I felt all was lost, that life for me was over

With your patience and love you gave me hope of life again

Before you entered my life I was stumbling and fighting for every breath

When you held me in your arms I could feel a rush of hope again

A feeling I knew I had lost, the dreary world I was walking in became renewed

As our love grew, I knew there was life to live again and love to feel once more

Time has passed since the day we began this love we share, each better than before

Where hope and contentment have replaced despair and strife, I am renewed by this love

You pulled me from the depths of sorrow and pain and showed me love as never before

I awake each day and look at you and see the sun rise in the sweetness of your smile

Why did it take so long for you to enter my life I struggled to find peace of heart and mind

Showing me that I was worth more than I thought of myself, I finally feel worthy of love

The sweetness of this love we share is better than the sweetest honey, golden and fresh

The warmth of your arms around me warms me even in the coldest of nights

The glow of your smile towards me has given a light to guide me through our life of love

Musings by M

When all we have known is sadness of life. The broken dreams and love that walks away from us. Then one day someone enters our life and changes us. We begin to understand love and the feelings of love. Life becomes worth living for us. We smile more, we are changed by the love they are willing to give us. We can finally live a life of love. M

Time Before You

Time before you, it was something I had to bear to gain another day

Now there is not a moment that goes by when I don't think of you

When I long to be with you and hold you in my arms

Time before you, it was filled with emptiness and hopes of love and joy

Once I met you, I knew I had found the one I wanted to live life with

To experience love, real love for the first time in my lonely existence

Time for you, it was heavy and burdensome until you came to me that day

We embraced and found within each other a life worth finally living

To share in our love the joys and hopes of tomorrows filled with our love

Time before you, I lived in solitude and chose to part from the world around me

To not see the joys of life without a love to call my own, shared with someone

Now I see the beauty of love, I know the joy of having someone by my side

Time before you, time spend in the shadow of self-doubt and deep sorrow and pain

Yet when I looked in your eyes there was love and joy, you said I love you for the first time

Never looking back, for fear I will lose you, I look ahead at our life as one in love

Time before you, seems like a lifetime ago, never to return to me with you here with me

It feels so warm and safe within this love we share for one another, joys I had only dreamed of

You brought life back into my heart, joy into my days, hope of tomorrow and love

Musing by M

We all know that love with someone who makes everything just feel right. Someone who shows us the changes we can make. Finding the life we have always wanted. We become a different person. Our friends ask us what has changed. They see the changes in us. Love, the feelings for and with someone special and amazing does that in us. M

Reminiscing

I was up all-night thinking and reminiscing of the day you entered my life

That day was the first day of me really living the life I always wanted to live

A day that seems like it was a lifetime ago and as if it was yesterday combined

As I thought of the beauty that entered my life and the love we share, I am in awe of you

From the inside out you are love and grace, someone I never want to lose, my forever

The one person who has seen to the depth of my heart and discovered love within

I sat in the dark and thought of you and this love we share between us, you still amaze me

Someone like you, loving someone like me, giving and caring the way you do

I don't deserve a person like you but thank all the powers above you are still mine today

In the darkness I heard you breathing as you slept next to me, thankful you love me

The softness of your body as you laid there, seeming to be dreaming of things you love too

I am so amazed, even now, that you gave your heart to me to hold, and I cherish every moment

As I sat there, I knew that I was the luckiest one alive to have you by my side, my love

To feel the power of this love I hold deep within for someone so beautiful I adore you

Thank you for loving me and giving me the life I have always wanted to share with someone like you

Musings by M

It could be a chance meeting or a date and you find the one who changes your world. Life before seems to fade away as love grows between you. Life begins for one or both of you in that moment and love begins. A year or a decade later as you are still so much in love, there is nothing can break you apart. That is when you know what true love is. M

Hope of a Life of Love

A wash in a place where life and love intersect for me

Your love brought me to life, now my life is the love we share

Never thought someone could become as important to me as you

When life gave me no hope of happiness your love has opened my heart

Not always easy to love, you have looked beyond my lack of hope

Time with you has changed me and opened a new world to me

There is a new way I see life and love now, because of your love for me

Your love has changed me from my heart out, beyond my past to our future

I am looking at life differently, a happy future within this love we share

Awash in the glow of a love to last the tests of time is ours to have

When I am with you I am the happiest I have ever been before

Thank you for loving me and giving me a hope of a life of love

Musings by M

A new love, new life of hope. All seems right in the beginning of love. There are times it takes work to maintain the love we fell for another, but it is worth it. M

Take My Hand and Walk With Me

Take my hand and walk with me, not in front or behind me, walk beside me

Holding on to the love we share is the life I want to live with you my love

Walking side by side holding on to the feelings and emotions we share

Take my hand and walk with me, we are one in this love of ours

When our love began I saw a future filled with passion and compassion

A life lived for the other, yet never losing who we are, together on our love

Take my hand and walk with me, as life is lived, and our love grows

Giving us the time to always see the other in our dreams of our tomorrows

You have helped me find courage to face each day with you by my side

Take my hand and walk with me as we move from year to year together, side by side

When I am weak you are there for me as I am there for you through every day we face

Together we are stronger than when we were apart, life is lived in the love we share

Take my hand and walk with me as the storms rage around us, safe in each other's arms

The shelter from the storms, we stand and protect the other through life's trials

Facing them with strength from each other, we will conquer the fears of tomorrow

Take my hand and walk with me, our past will soon fade away, the memories of before

Tomorrow is brighter than our yesterdays as we hold each other's hand, strength in our love

We give to the other the courage we have held for true love, as we walk hand in hand

Musings by M

In love we become partners in the life we seek to build. In a marriage or long-term relationship, we build the foundations of love and support for each other. Life has its ups and downs but 2 people can grow and prosper side by side and hand in hand. M

the Greatest Mystery

The greatest mystery of life is how we can fall in love with another

When there are billions of people throughout the world around us

We feel the draw to another without any thought of another

Life is full of mysteries but the biggest of them all is love

Feelings grow in an instant or over time, but love will grow

Usually when we least expect it to happen it happens to all

Love will grow with the least likely to love each other but it does

And people wonder why it happens, but love will always find a way

A mystery to last the ages is the feeling of love for another person

Allowing our love to grow, even in the hardest of hearts it will bloom

Softening and changing hearts in all who allow love to grow within

The feeling can be overwhelming to some, soothing to others

When there are billions of people throughout the world around us

We can feel the draw to just one person without a thought of another

The Greatest mystery of life is how we can fall in love with just one person

Musings by M

Love is the greatest mystery of life. We fall in love with no explanation. M

My Thoughts of You

My thoughts of you and thoughts of us together are cherished thoughts

I have never met someone like you before and I found peace in your arms

A peace I had never known before the day our life was joined as one in our love

My thoughts of you warm me even now remembering the love we have shared so long

No one ever allowed me to be me until you came into my life and let me love you

From that day on I knew there was going to joy and happiness for all my life to come

My thoughts of you have brought to me a wonder I had never known before we fell in love

Through all my days before you, I was lost and never felt connected to anyone like we are

I was alone in my quest for love to last the ages and help me change into the one I am with you

My thoughts of you bring a smile to my face whether you are near or far away from me

The way you make me feel each day is fresh every day, we were destined to find our love

Never leave me my beloved, let us grow old together, let our life in our love flourish more every day

My thoughts of you, I never knew what real love could feel like until I heard you say you loved me too

The waves of emotion as I think of you have carried me even through my days that have been dark

The light of your love for me, the hopes and dreams of every tomorrow seen, are in my thoughts of you

Love can change us. For better or worse is said at weddings even now. When love, a real love is found, life and love have finally merged to make everything better, even during stressful times life can throw towards us. Having someone stand with us makes it easier to get through the struggles. M

Just a Call Away

A ll you have to do is call me and I will come to where you are

Our friendship is greater and deeper than just friends

From the day we were kids and every day since, you are more to me

I hear your voice and peace settles over me, nothing can hurt me

I hope I am the same for you, our friendship goes beyond all others

We have been through so much together and away, but here we are

You are so important to me, and I know you feel the same way about me

If anyone tries to hurt you, I will stand up and protect you, you are safe with me

And I know if I need your help, you will stand up for me too

Never too far from each other even if you are in a different place and time

Our bond has withstood fights and disappointments never broken

I have your back, and you have mine, side by side we stand and fight for each other

We met when we were young, even though we are different, our friendship is the same

Strong and unbreakable, even though there are so many that have tried

If they want to hurt either of us, we will defend each other against the world

Musings by M

We all have that one person who is our go to, our ride or die. We grew up together, but let months or years go by with no contact, we get a phone call, and it all picks up were we left off, a lifetime friendship. M

Ease of Loving You

L ife has never been easy for me; I struggled to make
sense of it all

Then one day something happened to change it all for
me

Someone entered my life and showed me the way to
understanding

The ease I feel in loving you took all my struggles away

Life never made sense before, it was like I was watching
from a distant shore

Everything seemed to pass me by, as I watched life unfold

But now it all makes sense, the doubts have faded away from my heart

Filled now with the ease of loving you, I found my way with you

Life was always a battle I never seemed to be able to win, defeated every time

Then you entered my life and helped me find the courage to face another day

Never sure I would ever vanquish the hosts arrayed against me from the start

Courage came from the feelings of love between us, you eased my heart and mind

Life, even now, has its ups and its downs, but I no longer fear them

With you by my side I can fight and conquer all my fears

My life has never been the same since you came into my life

Within the ease of loving you; my child, you have given me a reason to fight

Musings by M

We have always had to fight fear since we were kids. Then one day someone helps us finds the courage buried deep within to fight for ourselves and them. Through the struggles there is also an ease we feel within. As we look into the eyes of our child finding strength and courage to face one more day, one more hour or just one more minute.

M

Within This Love

Never before and never since have I met a person who compares to you

While I have searched the world over, there is no one like you alive

An angel sent from the heavens, a soul so full of life and love for others

There is only one like you and anyone lucky enough to find your heart is blessed

They will never be the same again, once they know you from the depth of their souls

Changed forever, they will see the world through your eyes

When I met you, I didn't understand the changes you would bring to me and my life

I was never able to understand why the world was so rotten and distorted from my view

Yet when I met you, my view of the world changed and became one of clarity and calm

You have changed me for the better, just your voice can change me dark day to sunshine

My heart leapt when I saw you for the first time, as if it finally came alive

Knowing you has created in me a person that can no longer look to my past pain and sorrow

Only a future that is better than before, a life to live within this love I feel for you my child

Your love for me has changed me from the core of my soul to shine this love toward the world

There is a hope I have never known as I hold you in my arms, your smile lights me way

When a child is born, they change the world around them. Their smile, giggle, a hug can turn the world upside down. From sad to happy, sorrow to joy. A child's love is pure and angelic. Yes they are work, but the work is the best work you will ever do. M

A Dream

I once had a dream that I wasn't me and that this wasn't my life

No one used me to become someone else as they pushed me away again

There was a smile on the face of the person who I saw in my dream, a happy person

I woke up and ran to the mirror, hoping to find that person standing in front of me

But when I looked I realized it was only me staring back, tears began to fall

I went back to my bed, and fell back to sleep, hoping to find that person again

As I slept I had another dream one where I was the center of my own life but not alone

Where people would say they were happy to see me and tell me they loved me

I smiled in that dream I felt alive and loved for the first time in my life, I was wanted

In the morning, I went to look in the mirror again and I realized it for the first time in my life

I could be the love to others that I sought to find in someone else, not alone anymore

You are the person I have been searching for I said to the person in the mirror

When we love ourselves and understand who we are to us, the love we seek will come to us

We will find the love we seek by showing love to others they will be drawn to our light of love

Always find your inner peace and the world will see the love you have to share with others

Musings by M

There comes a time in all of our lives when we will realize there is a need to find ourselves as us. We should be good in our own skin and stop trying to be someone else. When we do, others will show us who we are. M

Sweet Embrace

Day after day I am amazed at the love I feel for you

Never in my life did I think I would find someone like you

I searched for a true, open, and honest love then you came into my life

From the day I met you, I knew I needed to find a way to help you love me

Never before had someone so amazing entered my life, the feeling of forever

I wanted to hold you in my arms and gaze into your mysterious eyes, captivating

When we finally found the feelings of desiring to get to know each other more

It seemed that we were standing all alone in an open space, no one around

As time went on there was a draw to always be with you, to touch you, to hold you

One day, however, we parted ways, the end broke me like never before

I have been lost since that day, I struggle to make sense of my life now

I want you by my side still, yet I knew you would find your way home to me

I stand and look at the distance, I hear your voice on the winds, I see your face

Never will I stop loving you, your love changed me, it helped me to heal my past

Now you are my past, I longed to see a future with you, I long for your embrace

Maybe, in the future, I will hold you in my arms again gazing into your eyes

To hear the sweetness of your voice again, hear the laughter and the cries of joy

But for now, I sit next to you, here upon the ground,
longing for your sweet embrace

Musings by M

We experience love, a profound love that changes
all of us differently. We have experienced loss. A
loss of love or a loved one. For some it has been
both. Someone who changed us from the inside out,
the one we will never forget. Allow for healing,
some never will heal from the loss. Some will. Each
of us have our own path to healing. M

The Wars We Face for Love

I awoke today from dreams of you and I but they were dreams of the wars we face

I looked out the window to the coldness of the day and chill rattled through me

There we were side by side, fighting the fight we have had for so many years to be us

Against the foe we have faced so many times before and must again, they continue

I awoke to the feeling of holding you in my arms while the world scoffed at us as we are

They never allow us peace to just be us, always trying to tear us apart, so much jealousy

They have never understood the love we share they seem to fear us and want to destroy us

Yet here we stand, side by side, the jeering and the yelling has made us stronger than their hate

I awoke from these dreams, dripping of sweat, as we fought to clear the way for this, our love

Never a moment of peace to be known, the battles rage all around us, broken and battered we fight on

Holding the other close, we continue to defend our right to be as one, against a world that hates us

You by my side and I by yours stronger than they know, yet exhausted from all the hate around

I awoke from our dream, as we parted ways to face the onslaught coming from all sides now

We raise our sword and shield, defending each other to the end, we shall not fail to win this war

You and I have always known the hatred of others for the love we share, yet here we are together still

The world will only judge and not know the strength we have as one, they fight to break our love

I awoke with you by my side, facing every battle together
we grow in strength, within this love we share

We stand united against a world set on trying to destroy
what we share, yet they never succeed in their quest

As we face them, we stand back-to-back dropping
everyone that is arrayed against us and our love

They try and try again to defeat us and tear us apart, yet
united in love we stand victorious

Musings by M

The world will judge us because of the person we love
sometimes. If that couple doesn't fit a view of what is
acceptable, they will judge and try to destroy that couple.
We love who we love and the world needs to leave the
couple alone. M

Why I Love You

Y ou asked me once why I love what was the reason I do

I looked at you and knew it was a serious question you asked

My response is not just one reason it is many reasons why

You brought the sun back into my life when we started our life together

When I had lived in the darkness of heartache and sorrow before you

Never knew what real love could be until you took my heart and loved me

You gave me hope again in the way that opened my heart to allow myself to love

There was never someone who showed me unconditional love before

Everyone before you showed me I needed to earn love to receive love from them

You showed me that words are important to the ones listening to me speak

That my words could be confusing to those trying to listen or read what I wrote

You showed me that I could show my inner self to others and share the love we share

You have always allowed me to just be me with all the cracks and imperfections

Giving me freedom to share my heart and mind with you and feel your love for me

Taking the fear of the past away and allowing me to believe in me and you

You took me into your heart knowing my past and the mistakes I have made before

Enabling me the freedom to love you openly and honestly, I have never known that type of love

When I make mistakes even now, you forgive me, and we learn to change things together

You asked me the reason I love you, there are many more reasons why I do

But this brief list is what I want to share with you to help you understand why

Just some of the reasons why I love you, because you are truly the one I love

Musings by M

We have had a talk with the one we love when they ask is why we love them. Have any of us struggled with the answer or answers? Sometimes it doesn't make sense to either one as the why, we just do. Be careful because the one asking honestly wants to understand why. Think of why and be ready to answer them, it will be an amazing moment in the relationship. M

It Was You

It was you that I needed to come into my life and show me

You showed me the way to open up to the world what was hidden

I was so afraid to let my word find a page to fall upon until you

It was you who showed me I could be more than a closet expresser of word or prose

Giving openness to feelings and emotions I buried deep inside my heart

You walked with me and encouraged me to open up to the world my love

It was you; it was always you that was meant to light the way for me one day

To take my hand and show me the way to tell my story for the world to see

The love I held from so many, yet you easily opened my words for all

It was you who gave me the strength to forge ahead and conquer my fear within

You encouraged me and told me I was more than who I thought I could ever be

Not facing the wrath, I had known before with your love you opened that door

It was you; your love has always given me courage to be more than I believed I could be

To put to page the love I feel within my heart and my soul, you are the one I needed

I could not have done this without you telling me I have always been more

It is your voice I hear in my head as I write telling me to continue on my path of openness

To share with the world the thoughts, emotions and love I feel within me every day

Placing words on page, writing what is inside of my mind and heart, my love for you

Musings by M

You entered my life and gave me the courage to openly share my feelings and emotions. I have always been told I was too silly a romantic to write anything, you told me I was better than that. You gave me the encouragement I needed to start writing again. It was you who emboldened me to share with others what was buried so deep within. It was you I needed to come into my life. M

Life Before You

All the struggles, the fighting myself to make sense of my life before you

All the frustrations and all the battles I fought to get here to you never made sense

Why did I have to go through everything I did before I met you almost destroyed me

All of it, all of the pain and the hurt I went through just to arrive to you were worth it

I understand now why it all had to happen to get me here to where you and I met

There were changes I needed to make to be able to love you the way you deserve

All the time I was being formed into someone who will take you to your fulness

When we met, the sparks were there never had I met someone like you

There was a feeling that we had met before, long ago and were meant to meet again

All the life I had lived and all I had lost cleared the path for me to finally find you

Together we are meant to face the world, side by side we will fight for the life we deserve

Without having to battle to make it to that day, I never would have been ready for this love

All the love we have shared has been something so sweet and so new to me, it shook me deeply

I have never met someone so amazing, so adorable, so deeply loving like you so perfect for me

A person who accepts me for me with all my flaws and weaknesses, yet loving me even so

All those years I felt alone and lost just wandering through life until you entered my life that day

I finally felt a love for someone who understands me who loves me the way you love me

We have been destined to find each other after so much pain and hurt, together we are made whole

Musings by M

Within all the struggles of life, heart ache and pain, molding us. We are being prepared to finally find a life and love that will last. All the brokenness of life and love can be healed with the one we finally find to love us and we can love through the healing. One day, one person will enter our life helping us heal the past and offer us change for a better future. M

Chapter Ten

Walked Through Fire

There is a feeling I get when I think of my past, some is good others are feelings of regret

I have experienced so much in my life much has taught me, some have hurt me and others

Words spoken actions taken by me and by others have affected me greatly in my life

My past is shrouded from many who know me, I have hidden it to keep me safe from it

Things that could have destroyed me, but a fighter to the end, I survived it all

Never want anyone I know and care about, to experience the things I have, the pain is still there

It was thought that I would not survive, but I am still breathing even now, fighting every day

Never one to give up on things I believe are right and true, I stand and wait for the next attack

So many others have experienced things in their lives that could have destroyed them too

I have walked through fire, stood in the storm, withstood the attacks of others against me

I will not give up on the fights I believe in, I will be weakened but will not be defeated

I was not supposed to survive to the day I am writing this, but I am still standing here

Life for me has never been easy, it is the same for so many others, here we stand against the pain

Never giving up on life and love, we fight every day to make sense of the trials and battles faced

When one ends another starts for so many, never a day of peace, days filled with battles to face

Yet so many continue to fight for life and love, just as I have done my entire life, at times defeated

But I will never give up on the people and ideas I believe are right and true, I will conquer the hate of others

They will again attack me, I will be required to defend my right to stand here today, walking through the fire

Musings by M

Walked through fire, facing many battles for heart and mind. A warrior's cry to the world possibly. A simple prose of courage, in the face of unsurmountable odds. We are all warriors and as warriors we fight for those we love and cherish, to keep them safe from harm and hate. Shielding them from pain. M

One

O ne step at a time, sometimes all we can accomplish is just one step a day

When the world and all the worries of the life we are living seems so heavy

Yet there is always tomorrow and the next day to plan for as we fight through today

One day at a time, never really looking beyond the day, we are facing it is our reality

Never realizing that there's something better for us down the next road we have to cross

It seems like today will never end because of all the struggles we are facing right now

One life for us to live, given a set number of days to find the love we crave, a life we want to live

At times things seem so distant from our grasp, wondering why we have to struggle so hard

Some call it Karma, some call it fate, some think the universe is just against them or a god hates them

One story for each of us, the story of a life lived or destroyed, the numbers on either side of the dash

A start date and an end date, what was between those numbers on a stone placed for others to see

A story of each person, will it be a horror, comedy or a love story, we choose the story line told to others

One step leads to another, followed by a life that was lived and love found by each person walking the world

Struggles come and struggles go, we learn as we move forward one step at a time, life and love with us

The story we leave for others to write of our existence is and has always been up to us to start

Musings by M

Life and love are taken one day at a time.
Everything we do will one day ne remembered by
those left behind. The dash between the numbers
say we were here. What will others remember of
us? What will be said of the dash on the stone?
M

My Wants

My wants are never given to me, always a struggle to make sense of it

When I seek guidance I am more lost than I was before nothing seems right

What am I supposed to do with my life so confusing to me anymore

My wants have been a fleeting wish for so long I have given up even seeking them

Always falling, it is getting harder to get back up and continue to push forwards

Struggling to find reasons why this continues to happen to me, wanting an answer

My wants, things I thought would make me happy, still just out of my reach, teasing me

Frustrations build up within me, not wanting to face another disappointment, but here it comes

Shaking in rage at what I have had to face every day, it has worn me out, I want to just give up

My wants have not been grand, they have always been simple, easy to manage for someone like me

I don't have many needs anymore, never needed too much out of life, but I still have wants

I believe in the powers that dictate life here, but I just want them to grant me a few things

My wants are mine, many never will know what they are, I don't share with others, because theirs aren't mine

Often times they are wants for others, those I love and cherish, wanting for them is who I am asking

I don't need much, just seeing others happy makes me the happiest because they deserve them

My wants, hopes and dreams have faded for me, nothing will really change in me, I want you to be happy

The smile on the face of a child, the love seen between two people who are in love, that is what I want

As life begins to fade within me, I want you to know what you all mean to me, I want this for each of you

Musings by M

Life is full of wants and desires. Some think they need to be big and glamourous wants. There are others who desire a simple life, one full of love and hope. A life filled with peace. They want those same things for the ones they love and care about. Simple hopes and dreams. M

So Tired of Fighting

I love you so much that at times it hurts deep within

I see you struggling with the pain of heart break it breaks me too

I know you need to face your pain, but I want to take it away

We have shared so much, but I know you have held back too

Knowing there is more you're afraid to tell me of what happened

But I will stand by you and walk with you as you heal the pain

The love I have for you is a love I have never known before

I hope you feel the same for me but only time will tell

Because the love I feel so deep within would destroy me if it ends

You have come so far and then take a step or two backwards into pain

It has fought to keep you so long; it can overpower you sometimes

I see it on your face, hear it in your voice, dragging you away from me

The love I feel within for you I hope can guide you to heal and leave the pain

But I also know you are so tired of fighting the past each and every day

I know you want to change but it has to be day by day finally winning your victory

When that day comes, we will look back at the path we have been on together

You will finally know peace; it will be a sweet and hard-fought victory

One day you will see who you have always been within my eyes

Musings by M

Those who have experienced the heartbreak of neglect and abuse spend a lifetime in pain, often masked behind a wall of anger, mistrust or humor, just to survive. Those experiences never go away. They become more guarded when love enters their lives, fearing yet again that they will be abused or mistreated. Loving someone who has been through this is difficult for everyone involved. The trauma is always present. But there is also hope for love to grow and flourish, creating a life filled with hope and security for both. M

When I Write

There are always doubts in the back of my mind when I write

Never sure if the words I place on page will be received as intended

Will they make sense to the reader or will they affect the heart within

I have hidden behind fear and doubt for years as I wrote the words I place

Sentence upon sentence written, does anyone want to know my thoughts

When I write the words used are intended to lift the heart of the reader

There are times the words written can seem sharp as a razors edge, cutting through

As my days pass by me and I wish the world will know the struggles of a simple man

At times I am shocked by the words I read when done, memories flow through the words

If anything, I have written affects another, it is something I am glad it has for you

If there has been something someone sees themselves in, it was meant for you

If brought up memories within the mind, I hope they have been loving memories

As I continue to write, as you continue to read what I put to paper is drives me

Giving me the desire to continue to write and share with others to read what I write

Never thought my thoughts would have any impact on others, thank you

Musings by M

Fear and doubt has kept so many stuck in a lane of life that keeps us comfortable. I was there with them. Writing in secret, not sharing with too many people, just a hidden passion to express who I am and how I felt. It took events in my life to change what comfort meant to me. Sometimes it takes what is needed to change the lane we are in.

M

People Who

P eople and places from my past have passed through my mind today

The people were family, friends and loves from years ago to now

They have all given me experiences and memories to hold on to even now

Some have made me smile, some have brought old hurts and pain

People who have walked with me through the highs and lows of my life

They stood with me and showed me that there was always a way to go

Either forward to new adventures or to turn away and find another way

Lessons learned some harder than others, I said goodbye to many along the way

People who will remain within my memories, thoughts of them can lift me when I am down

However, there are some who taught me tough lessons as well, of whom not to trust

Lessons that were hard on me, but needed to get me where I am today, making me strong

Finding a balance between hope and sorrow, between love and hate, to become me

People who have influenced me, who have given to me valuable insights into my own heart

That showed me that there are times in my life when it is best to be alone, to think and ponder

Giving to myself, learning to like myself after hating me for so long, feeling I was worthless

Thinking I had no value, many left me standing in the sadness of my life, I thought I was him

People who have stood by me encouraged me to fight for a better day, for a better life than I had

Enabling me through their examples to see the richness of a life well lived, through my struggles

Giving me the strength to rise again from the depths of the well of sorrows I used to be in

Climbing out I was able to finally stand in the light of a life I had always hoped for but never found

People, whom I call friend and family, those that showed me that there is always a way to find oneself

To look at life, not through rose colored glass, but in the stark reality of a life that builds one day to the next

Through all the struggles, through all the joys, through all that life can drag us through, I am just me

Thank you all for the lessons and the memories, for the love and the loss, without you, I would never have learned

Musings by M

People come and people go during our life's journey.
Others stay to help us through something. Some stay
throughout our lives. We do the same for others. When
you think back on the people you have had pass through,
what do you remember about them? Are they still around
or are they no longer there? Did they leave good memories
or bad ones? Who are they and do you hope they return?

M

Who Is This I See

W ho is this I see in the mirror today far from the child I used to see

Where did he go, why is he lost to me now, I wonder where life is for me

I long for him to return to share the joys of a young life together

Who is this old man I see; he has gray and lines and aged before me now

The blond hair has been replaced with silver and gray, some has even gone away

The eyes are still of the child I once knew, but he doesn't see the world the same

Who is this worn and weathered man standing before me in the mirror looking tired now

Where is the strength of youth once known when he'd face the day with hope

Now all I see is a broken and shattered old man staring back at me

Who said that life would be easy, they lied to me when I was young and strong

Now the toll of years of struggle and strife faced just to be here now

What passed for a life is not the one I placed my hopes and dreams upon when young

Who said that there would be golden years as the twilight of life approaches

When the strength of youth fades and the pains of what was lived follows me now

Who is this old man I see in the mirror today, I long for the child of my youth again

Life is never what we think it will be. We face loss and pain. We struggle to make enough to live. All the sports and the injuries we pass through when young can take a toll on us as we age. For far too many, the so-called golden years, are actually tarnished brass. The body begins to hurt and the strength we once knew fades with age. Live life, enjoy life, but understand we will all go through this process. M

Longing For

Longing for simpler times when the world appeared to be different to me

When the suffering of so many around me was not as apparent as it is now

Life for me was easy without the fear of a life losing so much I loved

Wanting those I love near me now, not sure why but I desire love and not hate

Have I gotten so old I cannot make things like they were before this change

But now I want to make things right with those I have so much love for

There are moments each day I want a simpler life, one filled with a childlike hope

When the future was an open book, unwritten by the hand of fate, a story to be told

Now it seems the pages have faded away and the book is quickly coming to an end

How did I get here, the chapters written by someone else, where is the story I wrote

When did time disappear where only memories of a story linger within my mind

It seems as if time has been unkind to me and only a longing of a simpler times remains

Musings by M

As we age and the years left seem to dwindle, we long for simpler and childlike memories to come to life. When the world was seen through eyes of wonder and hope. The older we get, oft times we become jaded by the life we have been through. We feel time slipping away, longing for the past more. M

Tortured

I have always been a tortured soul as I walked through my life

Never known peace in the common sense, always felt isolated from others

Not a part of the world, but something outside looking in towards the world

Standing alone I watch the world pass by me, no one staying near for long

Life as I see it is a place of joy and happiness in the faces of those I encounter

Yet so alone, a being left to the edge of life searching for real love

Looking through a prism of colors that shift with the winds of change all around me

It disorients me as I look through it, life is not what I thought it would be for me

Instead, I have been tortured, even when I tried to fit in, it was more pain than pleasure

Tortured within my heart and mind, I struggle to make sense of why it never works for me

Yet alone, I never need to fake a life that others expect me to live, I can be myself instead

Still, I have always wanted a love and a life where I could finally find true peace

This thing called life has been a tortured experience of hopelessness and sorrow instead

Never finding the love I have sought, instead I have been pushed outside, where I can survive

Others seem so happy, I have never known what that is, just a tortured soul is who I am

Musings by M

There are people who have a view of the world that is so mystical, so profound that they never truly fit in. Their view of life and love is almost other worldly. Where they see beauty and peace. Unfortunately, for those souls the world we live in never matches what they see and life becomes painful. They can become so sealed off from others that the world see them as hard and uncaring, even though they are only needing to protect themselves. Where do you fit into this world? Do you see beauty or ugliness? M

Within My Mind

Often my nights are spent deep within my mind and darkness settles in

What if I were to leave and never come back, who would miss my presence here

Would I be missed or just an afterthought like so many nights even now

Is there a reason I am still here after so many have gone before me

Will I been next or will I need to stand by that hole again saying goodbye to another

What is the purpose of me being here still, most nights I am alone in my mind

All I can do is sit here with a single light going to see my way around again

I have lost so much and so many, what is there left for me to do anymore

Time has not been kind to me, and I hurt everyday now, the pain within is hard

Never thought I would be lost like this as I grew older thinking there would be love

Yet I sit here alone, I wonder why I have to face another day after a night like this

Sleep eludes me most nights, closing my eyes only leads me to see more of the pain

I am done fighting for attention from anyone, I will be the recluse I have become now

Sealed off from the world and sitting here alone again tonight, no one near

I am going to stop chasing others and see who even cares if I am breathing or not

This became the inspiration by someone I met today who tried hard to be happy, but behind his eyes I saw him screaming for someone to see him. He longs for love and family. As we parted ways I told him I saw him, he stopped and turned back towards me and just looked at me for a couple of minutes before leaving. M

Facing the Evil Again

Sleep escapes me more and more as life weighs me down with sorrow

When my dreams are always of a fight I must face alone again in my soul

Never a moments tranquil rest, the battles rage around me still

Thoughts of those who I have lost to time and space, burdens even my sleep

When times of by-gone days appear, there is a race to be run to survive

Dreams for me have become nightmares, hate and pain are all around me now

I find no repose even within my dreams, as I face challenge after challenge alone

I awaken, shattered from the thoughts of all I have lost in this life, no one near me now

Alone in my dark room, it is the middle of the night, my heart racing from the fright

Facing all my foes from times past to times now, never finding solace in my dreams

There is nothing but destruction and despair, as I close my eyes again to the world

Hoping this time, I will find peace, but only finding battles at my feet

Time and time again, I scream for someone to rescue me from the battles I face alone

Yet no one comes to rescue me from the demons I must face as the nightmare comes again

I stand against them every night and fight this fight alone, facing the evil I feel all around me in my dreams

Life is never easy. Life can seem like there are battles to fight every day and night. When we cannot even sleep in peace, we become overwhelmed even in our dreams. Dreams become nightmares to those who go through this. Sometimes it is from past trauma, other times it is from something or someone else. The pain never goes away. M

Hidden Words

I don't know what I am doing anymore, so much has become confusing

When I attempt to do something, my mind wanders back in time to me and you

It is overwhelming at times, other times it causes my mind to stall in thought

I don't know what you are wanting to tell me when we speak you seem so guarded

As if there is something you are not saying, keeping what you want to say hidden

I don't want to think this way, but it is hard not to see and hear the hesitation

I don't know why you feel the need to hide anything from me, I have been open with you

Is it because of feelings you are afraid to share with me or are you hiding a secret from me

Are you in love with me as well or are you no longer wanting me in your life anymore

I don't know if you love me the way I love you, even when you tell me you love me still

Feelings I have for you have never ended, but I wonder if your love ended for me

Are we nothing or are we everything to each other, like we used to be for us

I don't know and it is killing me inside, the confusion is making me wonder every day

All the plans and hopes we once had seem to have been taken away by your silence

What are you hiding from me, have you lost your love for me and our future

Musings by M

When we know someone and we can tell they are holding back information that might hurt us, it can make is think all kinds of things. It is strange feeling things are being hidden. Always be open and honest with each other when you are friends or more. It will help keep the relationship strong and healthy. M

I Survived

I survived everything they tried to throw at me, never giving up on myself

Surviving the hate and abuse caused by people I once trusted

Now I know that I was never meant to have then in my life they were toxic

I survived to face another day to prove them wrong about me and here I stand

I have walked through fire to get here today, bruised but I am not beaten

All the hate I felt through the struggles I have faced made me stronger and fiercer than before

I survived them and their minions to look them in the eye and smile knowing they didn't beat me

I have suffered at their hand, but understand that I am better for everything they put me through

Never to trust like I used to trust, now I will watch where I place it, only for those who earn trust

I survived a life full of pain, inflicted by the ones who were supposed to love me for who I am

But they chose to abuse me instead, attempting to destroy me as a person, here I still stand

Giving up is not an option for me, walking through fire, I survived everything they did to me

I survived to live another day, then another turning into months and years, I am different yet still me

All they tried to do to me showed me they fear someone like me, I know the truth of what they have done

Standing here now, facing them and seeing the disbelief on their face, here I still stand with a smile

Musings by M

When someone goes through years of abuse at the hands of others, but never breaks from it, they survived. When they learn to love themselves and cherish each day of life, regardless of the hate from others, they are survivors. When someone does not become like their abusers, they are amazing and can love others better, because of all they have been through. I am proud of who you are. M

They Tried

They tried, all of them have done everything they could to you

They tried to break your spirit, to make you weak, they failed

They tried to terrorize your mind, causing you pain, they failed

They continue to try and destroy who you know you really are

The warrior spirit within you was passed down over the generations

They tried to destroy, but you are still standing to face them today

They tried, with everything they had, but you beat them each time

Their lies, their rumors, their words and actions sent to stop you, they failed

They tried to keep you from doing what you are meant to do, but again they failed

They tried with hate filled words, they slid off you like a rain in summer

They tried to make others believe the lies, those that know you knew the truth

They tried and continue to try to ruin your name, but your name is powerful

They tried but they failed to destroy you in the eyes of the world because they fear you

They fear the truth of you, they fear the power you hold in your hands, they fear love

They tried to change you, to kill the warrior within you, you have never failed your truth

Musings by M

There are those of us who seem to have to fight every day just to survive. They are the target of many around them. They seem to never find peace. When the world never leaves them alone, they can grow tired and many give up and let the world beat them down. Once in a while, there is someone who refused to give up. This is who this Musing was written for. Stand with your head held high and understand who you really are. M

When Fear Controls

F ear can overtake us when there has only been pain from love before

When life has been unkind to us, when everyone has hurt us

We fear to allow love in, we guard our hearts like we have learned to

Fear can cause us to lose the love we were meant to share with someone

After years of pain and sorrow, we begin to shut down to our emotions

Not letting love to even seep into our lives, sealed off to love

Fear can control us, as we watch for the pain to appear in any feelings we have

Reminders of the pain is stronger than the love we are meant to share with another

We turn our backs out of fear of being hurt again if we allow love to enter our hearts

Fear controls the broken heart, love can heal the brokenness and take the pain away

As we see the world through the pain from the past, we cannot see what love can be

Allow the love that meant to heal us, give love a chance again into heal our broken hearts

Musings by M

After a life of hurt and pain, fear can overtake us. When everyone let us down before, it is difficult to trust when someone new comes into our life. We become bitter and guarded by the life that was forced onto us. Which in turn causes us to protect and seal ourselves off from love or feelings for another. Try and give love an opportunity to show us someone is truly different and kind. This can be for kids of abuse to adults who have never been love unconditionally. M

Caged Within

I locked myself away from the world one day, I needed to feel safe

A day turned into weeks then months now it has been years locked inside

My fears have overtaken me, and I am now feeling as if life is done for me

Locked inside this cage, my mind has run free, there is no more pain

So many people have let me down, some have abused me, so I stepped away

To guard myself from all the hate that has been thrown onto me by others

I turned away from life and love and chose to hide within this cage, sealed away

I was so afraid of the abuse and pain that I couldn't stand the world outside

Locked away, my mind began to calm, the racing thoughts began to slow

Never had my mind been in such a peaceful state until I locked the door on my cage

Now I want to look outside again, to see if life and love can find me, is anyone true

But fear of the unknown still haunts me even within this cage I created for myself

I looked to others to make me whole, I looked to others to love me, never loving myself

Years have gone by for me, as I have stayed locked within the cage of my mind, now I feel alone

I long to find trust again, not just in others but also within myself to love a life I dreamed of

But each time I try and venture out, the fear has overtaken me, and I stay deep within

Musings by M

When someone has been through a lifetime
of abuse they can go either way. They can
either turn into the abuser to make them feel
better or retreat and never trust another
again. Either way they act, it will cage them
in. M

The Weight

Losing you is the worst day of my life, such a heavy weight of sorrow

Losing you weighs my mind down into the depth of my soul

Leaving all my hopes and my dreams torn and shredded on the ground

The weight of your loss, like a boulder around my shoulders, unbearable

Weighed down by the pain of knowing you will not ever be mine

The love I feel, the desire I feel for you, it is more than I can bare

I have lost the one I searched for my whole life; you are the one

Someone I saw myself with until the end of my days, lost to me now

Life will never be the same, the weight of my sorrow is too much for me

How can life go on when the one I searched for so long is now gone

Times spent together flood my mind, the love has broken my heart now

Never will life be the same for me, you are gone from me never to return

Broken and battered by the anguish within me, life is gone to me

Your love brought me to life, losing you has weighed me down

I am breaking under this weight of knowing you are never returning for me

Musings by M

This one is not about me. It is, however, for anyone who has lost the love of their life. It can be a sudden divorce or life was taken and their love is now gone. Life is never the same, things have changed. Life can become dark and pain filled from the loss. I felt this within my heart as I wrote, for whomever it is meant to reach, may you find healing. M

Until I Am Home

You all think I am doing okay even though I am lost today

You will never know the depth of the sorrow I feel within

I have learned that to survive this life, I need to fake it to you

I have decided to keep hidden the pain I carry with me today

Until I am home, and shut the world out of my loneliness

Not until I can keep from you the sorrow locked inside of me

You could not understand the way I feel every day I feel so alone

My days I put on a mask to wear in front of each of you

So, I can pretend to be whole, when I am really shattered within

You will never understand the pain and sorrow I carry deep inside

Without her here by my side, there is nothing left for me to live for

I have lost the one who helped me to be alive again, now she is gone

I will never be the same, life for me is over, I am a walking shadow nothing more

Until I am home, and shut the world out of my loneliness

Not until I can keep from you the sorrow locked inside of me

You could not understand the way I feel every day I feel so alone

My days I put on a mask to wear in front of each of you

So, I can pretend to be whole, when I am really shattered within

To protect you and not to interfere with your life, I wear a mask

The smile you see is painted on, the tears falling are unseen by you

If you knew the depths of my sorrow, you would never survive this

Weakness is not an option; I have to fight the urge to just give up

Until I am home, and shut the world out of my loneliness

Not until I can keep from you the sorrow locked inside of me

You could not understand the way I feel every day I feel so alone

Every day I put on a mask to wear in front of each of you

So, I can pretend to be whole, when I am really shattered within

The day she left me here to try and continue on with life, I died inside

Never to be whole again, I am hollow and lost to life and will never love again

That day they laid her to her final rest, I was destroyed, dead inside, beyond repair

I wanted to be with her, but she was ripped away from me the day she died

Musings by M

This is written in a song style or format. I have known many people who have lost loved ones over my life. I have seen and felt their loss. When we lose the love of our life, it can be devastating. That could be a spouse or a lover and it could be our closest friend. Whatever the loss, it changes all of us and the world expects us to be okay, on their time frame. It always takes time. M

As the Battles Rage

P eaceful dreams are what I seek to have as I sleep at
night

Yet what I find is terror and destruction of life and love
within

Is it a warning of what is to come or is it just a deep
thought feared

Quiet is how I want my mind to be, but it never seems to
be that for me

Always looking for a place to hide, from the chaos of the world around

Yet my life is full of so much that screams at me, no place is found to hide

Tranquil is what I want my life to be, but there are battles to fight each day

As I open my eyes after dreams filled with terror, there is no turning back for me

As each battle is brought to me to face, my only choice is to fight again

Empty of the life I seek for me and for others around me, yet only chaos is found

Devoid of the screams from within each of us, only battles to be fought to live

Away from the noise and terror felt, yet there is never peacefulness found within

Seeking is the life I live, peace is far away, quiet is sought but only screams are heard

Tranquility is desired but only emptiness is felt deep within the hearts and souls of each

Never to be found as the battles rage around, fighting is all that is known

Oftentimes, nightmares come to us, they can be deeply hidden feelings or emotions, some are experienced to show us that we need to be careful of someone or something. Other times they are a fear od something we hold inside during our waking hours. Dreams can be of our hopes, desires or wants. These show up in dreams of something sought or hoped for. Or of something lost to us. What do your dreams bring to you? M

In the Stillness of My Room

As I sit here in the stillness of my room alone with the memories of you

I can feel you close to me and am reminded of what we once shared

As they fade from my mind, I will be reminded in the words and photos on my walls

As the life I have had thrusted on me begins to overwhelm me, memories flow in

I have lost so much over the life I have been given but you are the hardest loss of all

When I thought life would be so different for me and you, time was never ours to hold

Sitting here in the stillness of my room I long to just speak to you again and laugh with you

Yet now that is no longer mine to enjoy and only the memories can fill the void for me

Gone are the times we shared never to add to the sounds of laughter and fun we shared

Time and time again I am reminded of who you have become to me in the memories I hold within

I cherish every word spoken by you now, I want to just hear your laughter ringing in my ears again

Now all I have to hold onto are the words and photos hanging on my walls in my room

Sitting here in the stillness of my room a tear slowly rolling down my face not of sorrow but of memories

I feel lost without you by my side but also hear you telling me to move on that you are here for me still

To the end of my days you are never forgotten, even in the faded memories of the laughter we once shared

I will see you again when I finally face my last breath upon this place we call home reunited with you

And it will be as if time and space were never between us as we revel in the laughter and joy once again

Until then, I look at the words and photos upon the walls as I sit in the stillness of my room

Musings by M

When love or life come to an end, we are left with only memories of what was. We can find solace in photographs and words written by the one we lost. We feel the pain of the loss and with it comes a time to mourn the loss. The we can begin to rebuild our lives again. For some, there will never be a time of rebuilding, just mourning. We should all be gentle on ourselves as we heal at different times and spaces. M

If I Had Known

If I had known how things would end up the way they did

I would have still fell in love with you, even knowing heart break was coming

You changed me for the better, even though it has been a pain filled lesson

If I had known that our life together would be so amazing at the start

But ending us with brokenness and heartache, I would have loved you still

I never met a person like you before, so amazing such memories I have of us

If I had known that the laughter and the jokes would come to an end for us

I would live them all over again, so much love and life we experienced together

Times of sadness and loss, we held each other, getting through it, side by side

If I had known one day you would build a wall between us, leaving me alone

I would still have given you my heart to break and my soul to shred to pieces

The time we had was the best times I have ever had in my life within a love

If I had known, I would lose you, I would still give you all the love I still have for you

Life is never going to be the same for me because I found love in your arms

A love that changed me, showing me that I can learn to love unconditionally

When there comes an end to things in life, we oftentimes mourn the loss and forget about the blessings we received during the time we had together with someone. When we only allow the sorrow to fill the void left, we can rob ourselves of the joys, love and laughter once felt. We will miss the ones we loved, it doesn't change the times we shared. "If I had known" came from those memories and thinking of how they changed me.

Wrong Side of the Bed

I wake up on the wrong side of the bed every day anymore

It doesn't matter if it's the left or right side of the bed, I am alone

You are not here with me anymore, everything feels wrong

In my dreams I can still see you, our life was so amazing together

But now when I lay down, there is no one beside me you are gone

Years we shared and lost to me in the blink of an eye, I am alone

I can still feel you close to me, but I know you are not really there now

Why did you have to go away, I am lost without you by my side

I long to hold you in my arms again, but you are not able to come home

The day I got the call, the voice on the other end was strained and nervous

They told me what had happened to you, and they were fighting to save you

My heart beating through my chest I raced to where they said you were

Arriving, I was met with sad and pitiful faces, as I was led to be with you

I begged and demanded that they save you, but there was nothing they could do

Taken from me now, I slumped to the floor as anguish overtook me

Now, I wake up on the wrong side of the bed every day anymore

It doesn't matter if it's the left or right side of the bed, I am alone

You are not here with me anymore, everything feels wrong

Musings by M

This Musing is deep and dark. It speaks of losing a loved one to tragic circumstances. Please be prepared, as it may trigger. As a personal note to the reader, I have personally experienced that contact. M

Silence Between

Silence between us has me questioning everything I ever thought about us

When once we talked for hours about everything that we could think of

Now there is silence, words left unspoken, feelings not expressed, just a void

You are the love of my life, the one I want to grow old with, what happened to us

What has caused the silence we now have between us,
are you tired of my love

Or is it the struggles we have been through the hurt the
world has caused us

Within the silence I find words just floating around,
questions I want to ask you

Do you love me still or has your heart hardened towards
me and the love we share

Why are words no longer spoken? Are you hiding your
hurt or your love for me

Your voice has always been the music of my life, the joyful
song of happier times

Yet now it seems the music and song have faded from
your lips into the silence we have now

I long to hear your voice again, to sing the songs of our
love and the plans we have made together

Where once was this happy couple, so deeply in love, the
joys and passions we felt for life and love

Now has become a valley between us, the distance
seems to be growing wider with every day

All I have wanted is this love we have shared, has it faded
within you now, never to be felt again

Come back to me my love, share the joy of love and life again with me, or is it too late for us

I long to listen to the song of your amazing tales as you speak of life and the love we share

Don't turn from me and leave me here alone, I cannot live with the silence we have now become

Musings by M

A voice, a word, spoken with the voice of music and song. A love shared between two, once so strong and alive, not lays dormant and no longer savored by two. Yet there is still a spark between them, even though silence is all they have. Words left unspoken, a void where tales of life and love once rang through the halls. Is it hurt or maybe pain, possibly it is the absence of love that now silently echoes between them. M

Ripped Away

Ripped away from me, you stole it and ran away from me why now

Why when we have been through so much and survived it all before

Now, why now did you run away from everything we have built

Ripped apart the foundation of a hope we had created with love together

Crumbling down now, destroyed by others or was it you who did it to us

Was there a reason for ripping it all down, why did you need to do that to us

Ripped asunder in mere seconds after years of careful building and support

There is only a pile of brokenness left to me now, thoughts are racing as to why

Never again to bask in the wonder of all that we created, ruined by rumors and lies

Ripped apart, but is it beyond repair, is there anything we can do to fix this now

We have survived so much before this, but what is to come of us? Do you even care?

So much put into building the foundation of our life together, gone in the blind of an eye

Ripped and torn, tattered pieces lay all around us now, is there any hope left to us

Do we try and fix this, if it's even possible, or do we start new, building a stronger foundation

Is there a chance, are you willing to find the strength to get beyond this or is it too late

Musings by M

This actually popped into my head while watching a video of a construction crew tearing down a school. But it also brought up a question regarding relationships. As the world and situations, including broken hearts and hurt feelings creep into any relationship. When these are too much for one or both to overcome, what is next? Heal yourself and heal the relationship. Speak to each other with love and respect. Life is difficult enough without the loving support of a partner, friend or our family. M

Distorted Truths

The world loves to paint a picture of what they see in each of us

Their view of us is not always the real us, some will taint us to feel better

Others will create their own picture, distorted and dark of who we are to them

People will only see us through the eyes they want to see us as, often times wrong

They will do everything they can to make the world decide we are the distortion

Never telling the truth of who any of us are as a person really, just what they think we are

Some will try and defend themselves, just to be mocked and lied about to everyone else

No matter how hard they try to change another's viewpoint, they are already distorted by lies

People suffer in a world that has a distorted view, having to fight just to be seen in their truth

When that becomes a reality, it can change a person into the distorted truth over time

Placing a mask to be what the world thinks they are, just to survive through each and every day

Then the world will mock them even more, pointing to the mask and making that the truth

Fighting for the truth is not an easy task in a world that only believes their own lies

Become better and stronger in our quest to show the world the truth of who we are to ourselves

Never let the world tell us that we are not who we know we truly are to ourselves and those who know us

We should all be true to ourselves and the person
we know we are, staying that person is our strongest
weapon

The world cannot change who we are, if we hold to the
truth, no matter how hard they hit us with the lies

Don't give up the truth, allow it to be seen by all, even
those who have a distorted view of their power

Musings by M

*People that fear the truth will distort it. They will claim falsehoods
and call them truth. When that happens, if we know the truth and can
prove it, stick to the truth, no matter what they may try. It is difficult
and will wear most people out but be yourself. Some in society have
said things like "that is your truth" but there is truth or non-truth in
life. I didn't say absolutes, I said truth or non-truth. When some
only see absolutes, it can block the truth. M*

About the author

Tucked away in the peaceful Black Hills of South Dakota, **Matthew A. Cone** finds both solace and inspiration in the natural world around him and the enduring love of his life. His writing is shaped not only by the beauty of his surroundings, but also by the raw experiences of living—moments of joy, seasons of loss, and the hard-won lessons that come with struggle.

What began as private journaling to make sense of swirling emotions has grown into **Musings by M**, a heartfelt series of writings that resonate with readers across the world. Through this ongoing collection, Matthew has crafted more than 860 musings—each one a window into the triumphs and trials of love, healing, and human connection.

The *Illuminations of Love* series has become the centerpiece of his work:

Volume I introduced readers to his deeply personal style of free-form verse, reflecting on the beginnings of love and its power to transform.

Volume II carried that journey forward, exploring resilience, heartbreak, and the discovery of strength in vulnerability.

Volume III now continues the story, offering an intimate exploration of love's many dimensions—romantic, spiritual, and restorative.

At the heart of Matthew's writing is his *Muse*—the remarkable woman who reignited his passion for the written word. Her belief in him, her inspiration, and her presence live within the pages of every volume. Many of his most cherished musings are dedicated to her, celebrating how love itself can heal, encourage, and create.

Matthew invites readers to not only experience his words but to reflect on their own stories through them. Whether you are in the midst of love, walking through heartbreak, or searching for hope, he hopes you'll find echoes of your own journey within his musings.

www.ingramcontent.com/pod-product-compliance
Lightning Source LLC
Chambersburg PA
CBHW051413090426
42737CB00014B/2643

References

❖

Steven H. Gifis, *Barron's Law Dictionary: Third Edition* (Hauppauge, NY, Barron's Educational Series, 1991)

Frances A. Schaeffer, *No Final Conflict: The Bible without error in all that it affirms* (Westmont, Illinois, Intervarsity Press, 1979)

Brennan, William J. Jr., "State Constitutions and the Protection of Individual Rights." *Harvard Law Review* 90 (1977): 489-504

Alfred Lansing, *Endurance: Shackleton's Incredible Voyage* (New York, Carroll & Graf Publishers, 1999)

Robert H. Bork, *Slouching towards Gomorrah: Modern Liberalism and American Decline* (New York, ReganBooks/HarperCollings Publishers, Inc., 1996)

Robert Shapiro, *The Search for Justice: A defense Attorney's Brief on the O.J. Simpson case* (New York, Warner Books, 1996)

Dinesh D'souza, *What's so Great about Christianity* (Washington D.C., Regnery Publishing, Inc., 2007)

Albert Barnes, *Barnes' Notes on the New Testament* (Grand Rapids, Kregel Publications, 1962)

Federal Rules of Evidence, 2009-2010 Edition (New York, West Publishing Co., 2009)

Bryan A. Garner, *Black's Law Dictionary: Third Edition* (New York, West Publishing Co., 1933)

West's Florida Probate Code with Related Laws and Court Rules (New York, Thomson West, 2008)

Edwin E. (Buzz) Aldrin, *Magnificent Desolation: The long journey home from the moon* (New York, Harmony Books, 2009)

George T. Nierenberg, *Say Amen Somebody* a screenplay documentary published in 1983

Cases

❖

Roe v. Wade, 410 U.S. 113 (1973)

McCreary County v. ACLU, 545 U.S. 844 (2005)

Van Orden v. Perry, 545 U.S. 677 (2005)

Marbury v. Madison, 5 U.S. 137 (1803)

Engel v. Vitale, 370 U.S. 421 (1962)

Miranda V. Arizona, 384 U.S. 436 (1966)

Michigan v. Long, 463 U.S. 421 (1983)

Loving v. Virginia, 388 U.S. 1 (1967)

Butchers' Union Co. v. Crescent City Co., 111 U.S. 746 (1883)

Ray v. William G. Eurice & Brothers, Inc., Md. Ct. App., 201 Md. 115, 93 A.2d 272 (1952)

Greiner v. Greiner, Kan. Sup. Ct., 131 Kan. 760, 293 (1930)

Ashcraft v. Tennessee, 322 U.S. 143 (1944)

Gideon v. Wainwright, 372 U.S. 335 (1963)

Douglas v. California, 372 U.S. 353 (1963)

Messiah v. United States, 377 U.S. 201 (1964)

Escobedo v. Illinois, 378 U.S. 478 (1964)

Berkemer v. McCarty, 468 U.S. 420 (1984)

Van Valkenburgh v. Lutz, 304 N.Y. 95, 106 N.E. 2nd 28 (1952)

www.ingramcontent.com/pod-product-compliance
Lightning Source LLC
Chambersburg PA
CBHW030930090426
42737CB00007B/379